Imaginative
Projects

A resource book of project work for young students

CAMBRIDGE
UNIVERSITY PRESS

Matt Wicks

CAMBRIDGE UNIVERSITY PRESS
Cambridge, New York, Melbourne, Madrid, Cape Town, Singapore, São Paulo

Cambridge University Press
The Edinburgh Building, Cambridge CB2 2RU, UK

www.cambridge.org
Information on this title: www.cambridge.org/9780521668057

First published 2000
5th printing 2006

Printed in the United Kingdom at the University Press, Cambridge

A catalogue record for this publication is available from the British Library

ISBN-13 978-0-521-66805-7 Resource book
ISBN-10 0-521-66805-0 Resource book

Contents

Map of the book

PROJECT	LEVEL	LANGUAGE FOCUS	SKILLS	TIME	ACTIVITY TYPE	TOPICS
Classroom language						
1 Creating things	elementary–intermediate	simple questions, names of classroom objects	speaking	15 mins	game	classroom language, art
2 Game play	pre-intermediate–intermediate	simple questions, instructions for games	speaking, writing	15–20 mins	gap fill	classroom language, games
3 Speaking	pre-intermediate–intermediate	simple questions, *will* for predictions	speaking	15 mins	questionnaire	classroom language, people
1 The island						
1.1 Island poster	elementary–intermediate	descriptions, modals of ability, prepositions of position	speaking, writing	60–90 mins	making a poster / map	travel, survival, geography, art
1.2 Travels with my rucksack	intermediate +	conditionals, modals of possibility	speaking	45–60 mins	team game	travel, survival, desert islands
1.3 Desert island students	pre-intermediate–intermediate	question forms, past verb forms	speaking	30–40 mins	discussion, ranking activity	travel, music, desert islands
1.4 Robinson Crusoe	intermediate +	narrative tenses, articles, reference devices	speaking, reading, writing	45 mins	text ordering activity	desert islands, survival, stories, famous people
2 Movie moguls						
2.1 The audition	intermediate +	adjectives and adverbs	speaking, pronunciation	30 mins	matching exercise, intonation game	media, people, drama
2.2 The mogul game	intermediate–upper-intermediate	media vocabulary, descriptions	speaking	45 mins	game	media, people, cinema, games
2.3 Movie magazine	intermediate +	reported speech, adjectives, superlatives	speaking, writing, reading	60 mins	reviewing movies	media, people, newspapers
2.4 Shooting	intermediate–upper-intermediate	instructions, direct speech	writing, speaking, reading	6–7 hours	making a film	media, crime, cinema, drama

PROJECT	LEVEL	LANGUAGE FOCUS	SKILLS	TIME	ACTIVITY TYPE	TOPICS
3 Space City						
3.1 Building the future	pre-intermediate–intermediate	comparatives, *will* for prediction	speaking	20–35 mins	vocabulary matching activity, brainstorming	cities, buildings, the future
3.2 The city of the future	pre-intermediate–intermediate	past tenses, *will* for prediction, descriptions	reading, speaking, writing	approx. 100 mins	reading, reading race, poster making	the future, cities, geography, art
3.3 Travel to Space City	pre-intermediate +	numbers, money, question forms	speaking, reading, optional: writing	50 mins	role play	travel, the future, drama
3.4 Loving the alien	intermediate	questions, general revision	speaking, pronunciation	40 mins	revision game	the future, alien game
4 The exhibition						
4.1 Three little pictures	pre-intermediate +	narrative tenses, optional: contrast and reporting verbs	speaking, writing	45–75 mins	describing events, drawing pictures	stories, people, art
4.2 Make my machine	pre-intermediate–intermediate	instructions, zero conditional	writing, speaking	90–120 mins	labelling a diagram, making a machine	inventions, science
4.3 Opening the wardrobe	elementary–upper-intermediate	descriptions	speaking	30–45 mins	describing pictures	fashion, clothes, people
4.4 Catwalk	elementary–upper-intermediate	descriptions, present continuous, colours	speaking	approx. 105 mins	putting on a fashion show	fashion, people, media
5 Blind date						
5.1 Getting a date	intermediate–advanced	second conditional, hypothetical language, questions		30–60 mins	role play, quiz	relationships, media, people, drama
5.2 The date	pre-intermediate–advanced	question forms, functional restaurant language	speaking, writing	40–90 mins depending on group size	script writing	food, relationships, people, drama
5.3 Photo love	intermediate–advanced	instructions, other areas as generated by students	speaking, writing	2½–3½ hrs over 3 lessons	making a photo story	relationships, media, people, art
5.4 Honeymoon	intermediate +	likes and dislikes, making suggestions, agreeing and disagreeing	speaking, reading	35–45 mins	discussion and selection game	travel, relationships

PROJECT	LEVEL	LANGUAGE FOCUS	SKILLS	TIME	ACTIVITY TYPE	TOPICS
6 Radio show						
6.1 Idols	intermediate +	question forms, past tenses, present perfect	speaking, writing	90 mins	interviews, research	media, famous people, fashion
6.2 Adverts	intermediate–upper-intermediate	present simple, *can* (ability), *should*	speaking, pronunciation	60 mins	writing and recording short texts	advertising, media, drama
6.3 The Harchards	intermediate	direct speech	speaking, writing	c. 105 mins	making a radio play	relationships, people, media, drama
6.4 Headlines	intermediate +	past simple, present perfect, reported speech	speaking, writing	60 mins	making a news programme	media, news, famous people
7 The restaurant						
7.1 Food families	elementary–intermediate	*Have you got? / Do you have? some / any*	speaking	25–40 mins	food vocabulary game	food, shopping, games
7.2 Setting up	pre-intermediate–intermediate	present simple,	speaking writing	90 mins	making a menu	food
7.3 Dining out	pre-intermediate–intermediate	polite requests, complaints	speaking	approx. 30 mins	role play	food, drama
7.4 Our restaurant	pre-intermediate +	hypothetical language, modals of possibility, decisions	speaking, reading	30 or 60 mins (two versions)	reading game	work, food, maths
8 Secret agent						
8.1 Equipping your agent	pre-intermediate–upper-intermediate	spatial prepositions, present simple, modals of ability, passive, *is used to / for …*	speaking, writing	60 mins	designing a poster	cars, spies, people, art
8.2 Codes	pre-intermediate–upper-intermediate	letters/alphabet, recent vocabulary	speaking writing	45 mins	cracking a code	spies, people
8.3 Interrogation	pre-intermediate–upper-intermediate	question forms, indirect questions, past simple, past continuous, present perfect	reading, speaking	60 mins	reading a newspaper, role play	spies, people, crime, drama
8.4 The base	intermediate	question forms, instructions, recent vocabulary, word order	speaking	55 mins	a game	spies, crime, games

PROJECT	LEVEL	LANGUAGE FOCUS	SKILLS	TIME	ACTIVITY TYPE	TOPICS
9 A midsummer night's project						
9.1 Introduction and background	intermediate or a mixed-ability class	past simple, past perfect, descriptions	speaking, listening	20 mins	Shakespeare quiz	famous people, media, theatre
9.2 Auditions	intermediate or a mixed-ability class	direct speech	reading, speaking	2½–4 hours	audition activities, script reading	famous people, stories, theatre, drama
9.3 Rehearsals and preparation	intermediate or a mixed-ability class	instructions, direct speech	speaking, reading, writing, listening	approx. 10 hrs	preparing for performance, making things	media, theatre
9.4 The performance	intermediate or a mixed-ability class	direct speech	speaking, writing	25 mins per show	performing a Shakespeare play	theatre, stories, drama
10 Time capsule						
10.1 Introduction	pre-intermediate +	modals of deduction, past tenses	speaking	60 mins	guessing game	history, people, geography
10.2 Decisions	pre-intermediate +	making suggestions	speaking	20–30 mins	planning activity	history, people
10.3 Filling the capsule	A, B, E: pre-intermediate C, D, F: pre-intermediate +	A: adjectives, spatial prepositions B: the future C, F: past simple, present perfect D: question forms E: narrative tenses, adjectives F: past simple, present perfect	A, B, C: writing C, F: reading C ,D ,E, F: speaking	A: 45 mins B: 30 mins C: 30 mins + 15 mins per lesson after that D: 60 mins E: 5 mins per student F: 90 mins	A: writing a description B: making predictions C: reading and writing diaries D: interviewing E: talking about photos F: making a scrapbook	A: geography B: the future, jobs C: stories, feelings, holidays D: people, jobs E: stories, families, people F: famous people
10.4 Burial	pre-intermediate +	prepositions of place	speaking, writing	30 mins	devising a ceremony	history, ceremonies, geography

Thanks and acknowledgements

Dedication
To Belinda, who read all these lines and saw what was between them as well.

The author would like to extend his sincere thanks to Nóirín Burke, Jane Cordell and Katharine Mendelsohn for their unflagging and tireless work on this tome.

The author and publisher would like to thank the following teachers and students who reviewed and pilot tested material from _Imaginative Projects_:

Ken Cooper, Okinawa Shogaku High School, Okinawa, Japan; Luiz Antonio Dentelo, Curitiba, Brazil; Lisa Eadon, the Bell Educational Trust, Saffron Walden, UK; Mark Hancock, Madrid, Spain; Rosie Hurst, London, UK; Samantha Lewis, the British Language Centre, Madrid, Spain; Natalia Lukina, 'Gasprom' Educational Centre, Moscow, Russia; Annabelle O'Toole, ILC, Hastings, UK; Nigel Pike, Cambridge, UK; Sean Power, Geneva, Switzerland; Ian Reid, Parede, Portugal; Joe Schmittgens, Freiburg, Germany; Wolfgang Voss, Droste-Hülshoff Gymnasium, Freiburg, Germany; Gaynor Williams, Ionina, Greece.

The author and publisher are grateful to the following illustrators and photographic sources:

Photographic sources:
Aquarius for page 37 (bottom); Camera Press/Gary Lewis for page 126 (centre left), /Jerry Watson for page 126 (top left); Corbis Sygma for page 37 (top left); gettyone Stone/Warren Bolster for page 50 (bottom); Ronald Grant Archive for page 126 (bottom left); People in pictures for pages 34 (centre left, right), 37 (top right), 77 (left), 126 (bottom right); Popperfoto for page 77 (right), /Reuters for page 34 (centre right); Rex Features Ltd for pages 34 (left), 126 (top right); Science Photo Library/NASA for page 50 (top), /Royal Observatory, Edinburgh for page 49 (bottom), /US Geological Survey for page 49 (top).

Illustrators:
John Batten; Hannah Davies; Tony Forbes; Ed McLachlan; Gillian Martin; Adrian Salmon, Katherine Walker; Gary Wing

Freelance picture research:
Hilary Fletcher

Book design:
Giles Davies Design

Cover illustration:
Carrie Bennett

Introduction

About this book

What is Imaginative Projects?

Imaginative Projects is a resource book containing photocopiable materials designed for supplementary classroom work. It is divided into ten units, each of which is aimed at motivating and encouraging teenage students.

Who is it for?

The book is written for teachers of English, whose students are aged between eleven and seventeen, and who are looking for new and original ways of presenting and using structures, vocabulary and fluency activities. It can be used to complement any coursebook, or to provide activities for special occasions such as the end of term or an arts and culture lesson.

How does it work?

Imaginative Projects is divided into ten chapters. The first eight of these are further divided into mini-projects. Each mini-project is a lesson on its own, and guidance is given in the teaching notes and the Map of the book as to which lexical / grammatical / skills areas it will focus on. This allows integration with the existing syllabus.

The mini-projects combine to form more extensive projects, which can be done over a period of time, allowing recycling of language and themes. Each of these projects has a Project guide at the beginning of its chapter, providing details of preparation, timing and level, as well as a box which gives specific information to assist in the successful completion of the project.

The remaining two projects, Project 9 **A midsummer night's project** and Project 10 **Time capsule**, are complete projects which cannot be broken down into mini-projects, but otherwise follow the same format as the other chapters in the book.

At the end of the book, there are two appendices, one on using new technology in project work and the other on using the community. Both are valuable resources when doing these projects. These are also referred to where necessary in the teaching notes.

Choosing to do project work

Why use projects?

Projects offer students a way of practising their English while having fun. They provide the teacher with opportunities for cross-curricular work, bringing in art, drama, geography, history and even maths (see the individual Topic area sections in the teaching notes for more details). By creating something, students use English as a tool and see how flexible and useful it can be. Most important of all, projects offer teenagers a chance to find their own voice and to do something meaningful and entertaining with the language they are learning. In short, projects motivate.

Which project should I use with my class?

There are several ways to choose a project. The simplest way is to select one that fits in with a particular topic area or language point. These are all listed in the Map of the book. For example, if you are studying vocabulary to describe the local environment, you could substitute or expand your coursebook exercise with the Island poster (1.1) from **The island**. Alternatively, a project can be selected to work on a range of skills, once again listed in the Map of the book. A teacher with a pre-intermediate class wishing to do some reading for detailed information might choose The city of the future mini-project (3.2) from **Space City**, whilst one wishing to practise fluency with upper-intermediate students could select Interrogation (8.3) from **Secret agent**.

Should I do the whole project or just a mini-project?

This often depends on the amount of time available in the class. If time is limited, it is sensible to begin with a mini-project. On the other hand, students often become so involved in a theme that they wish to follow it further: in this case it is easy to add on extra mini-projects from the same project that explore different skills. Almost all of the mini-projects in Projects 1 to 8 are designed so that they can be changed around and used in any order. Where there are exceptions, these are pointed out in the teaching notes.

Managing a project

How can I get my students interested in doing a project?

First, the project needs to be presented in a stimulating and enthusiastic way. Teenagers need to focus on a goal. In some of the projects, that goal will be the completion of the whole project (e.g. in Project 10 **Time capsule**, the burial of the box will motivate the students); in others, the goal will simply be the conclusion of a smaller micro-task (e.g. Project 8 **Secret agent**, where the students have to decode a text). In either case, the important thing is that the students know what the goal is.

In addition, students should be encouraged to take ownership of the project. Each project has introductory activities, and these should be augmented by bringing in realia (where possible) and being willing to construct an environment in which the project can take place. Teenagers are always keen to decorate their own 'space' at home, and doing the same thing at school should give them a similar sense of achievement and investment in the project. In Project 2 **Movie moguls**, for example, bring in a clapper-board (or make one out of cardboard), or pictures of film stars to stick around the walls. This will make the classroom look more like a studio. For Project 3 **Space City,** get hold of pictures of aliens from old movie magazines or comics and give students a dedicated area where they can build their city up lesson by lesson.

What can I do when they all speak in their mother tongue?

Once the project is under way, there is bound to be some L1 used as students get carried away with the tasks. A certain amount of this is acceptable, because it shows that they are involved in the project. However, there are a couple of ways to prevent it becoming a habit.

First find out why students are speaking in L1. If they are not using English to ask for scissors, to say things like *it's your turn* or to ask their partner simple questions, it probably means that they need a short reminder of some of the basics of classroom language. To this end, there are three activities at the beginning of the book, in the Classroom language section, to practise these areas. Each activity is short and can be used before a project or in the middle of one, if you find that the class are really over-using L1 for day-to-day things.

If students are being lazy when they know the classroom language well, you can take 'offenders' out of the project for a short while and make them add one or two phrases to a wall poster of classroom language. This builds up over time as more and more students add to it. It can also act as a reminder to other students to use English in the classroom.

What about the noise?

Noise may actually be a good sign, as it often means that students are engaged and enjoying what they are doing. However, if you feel it is having a negative effect on their work, develop a 'quiet sign'. This can be something as simple as raising a hand, or even clapping your hands. Once students recognise this signal, they will know that they are expected to be quiet. It is quite important to give students a reason to be quiet, as well. Each time you reduce the noise, ask one of the groups how they are getting on, or ask a quick vocabulary question. On other occasions, the quiet moments can be used to signal a change in the tempo of the class, maybe moving people from one group to another if the activity requires it, or reminding the class of how much time they have left. Above all, speak quietly and don't try to shout louder than them.

How can I integrate a project into the curriculum?

If you have chosen the project on structural criteria (e.g. by choosing the mini-project 5.4 **Honeymoon** to practise 'suggestions'), then the link can be made between a presentation in one lesson and the project as a free practice activity in the next. Alternatively, a project can be used as an end-of-term session, revising what has been studied earlier in the year. Get students to look at the grammar areas for homework so that they revise the structures before coming into the project.

If you have chosen to use a project because it presents new vocabulary in an interesting way, then it is a good idea to follow it up with a vocabulary revision exercise. This can be something from the existing coursebook which practises the same lexical set. On the other hand, you might like to avoid the coursebook altogether (or perhaps keep those exercises for homework or revision) and use the project as the presentation and one of the following ideas for practice.

1   Write down all the new words that students have learnt in a project on cards (or get them to do it). Put the cards into a bag. In groups, get them to make up a chain story. Give them the first sentence of a story. In turn, students take out one of the cards and continue the story using the word. If they cannot, then the story and the word pass on to the person on their left. If they can make a sentence, they get a point and the next person takes a different card.

2   Choose at random a word that they have learnt. Each student draws a picture that represents that word but does not write the word. Repeat this. Each time the students use a different piece of paper (so small pieces of recycled paper are ideal here). When you have given about five or so words, gather all the papers together, mix them up and hand them out. Write the words on the board. Divide the students into teams of four and give them about twenty pictures each. They then have to match the pictures with the word list. They should write their word under the picture. Inevitably, some groups will receive their own

pictures back, but this does not matter as the artists can be challenged by their colleagues if they feel the drawing does not accurately represent the word. It doesn't really matter whether or not they are correct, because the process helps fix the words in their minds. To complete the exercise, gather all the piles together. Then hold each picture up in turn and read out the word by it. The original artist can then say whether or not the group's guess was accurate.

3 Give confident students a card at random with a recently used word on it to use in a role play. Tell them that they are in an everyday situation and they have to use this word at least three times. Students then improvise the situation, reacting to the other characters' comments as quickly as possible. Situations which work particularly well are railway carriages, dinner tables and dates. This activity is short, easy to set up and endlessly entertaining, especially if the words are very diverse, such as 'steering wheel' and 'donkey'.

Creating things

Topic area
classroom language, art

Language focus
simple questions
names of classroom
objects

Key vocabulary
*stapler, pencil, tube of
glue, rubber, pair of
scissors, pencils, ruler, hole
punch, sellotape*

Skills
speaking

Level
elementary–
intermediate

Time
15 minutes

Materials
5 x classroom object
cards on page 14 per 4
students
classroom objects (to
illustrate meanings)

Before class

1   Photocopy five sets of the cards on page 14 for each group of four students in your class (so, 25 sets for 20 students). Cut them up.

2   Find real examples of all the objects on the cards (stapler, pencils, etc.).

In class

1   Hold up the objects or the Classroom object cards (from page 14) and elicit the name of each item.

2   Write the whole list on the board and check the spelling with the students. With stronger students, you can erase the words on the board before they begin playing.

3   Elicit expressions which students need when they want to borrow / use something that somebody else has got: *'Can I borrow your stapler?' 'Have you got any pencils, please?' 'Have you got a rubber, please?'* Write all of these up on the board.

4   Put the students into groups of four. Give each group five sets of cards and shuffle them together well (mix all five sets up). One of the students deals the cards to the others. Each student receives eight cards. The remaining cards are placed face down in the centre of the table.

5   Tell the students that the aim is to get a complete 'set' of classroom materials – in other words one each of the cards showing a stapler, some scissors, a pencil, some pencils, a rubber, a ruler, some paper, a hole punch, some glue and some sellotape (the list on the board). They do this by asking the person on their right a question: *'Can I borrow your ruler?'* or *'Have you got a ruler?'* The student who is being asked must then give the appropriate card, if they have it, to the first student, with the correct responses – *'Of course.' 'Yes, you can.' 'Yes, I have,'* etc. If the student does not have the item they do not have to give any cards away, but must simply say: *'No, I'm sorry you can't,'* or *'No, I'm sorry I haven't'.* With the lowest levels, write these expressions on the board. Alternatively, they may win by getting a 'trick' i.e. five of the same card (five staplers or five rubbers, etc.).

6   There is one additional type of card with a large question mark on it. This is the joker of the pack and is called the *'I'm sorry, I don't understand'* card. If you have one of these cards, you do not need to give any cards to your opponent, even if you have them. Simply put the question mark card on the table and say *'I'm sorry, I don't understand.'* The student who asked for the card gets nothing, and the student who had the question mark card puts it to the bottom of the pack in the centre of the table and takes the top card for him/herself.

7   The winner is the first student to get a complete set of all ten items.

8   If one group finishes too quickly, simply shuffle the cards and get them to play again while the rest of the class finish.

Follow up
Give each of the students a copy of page 14 and get them to label each card with the correct name so that they have a written record of what they have been doing.

CLASSROOM OBJECT CARDS

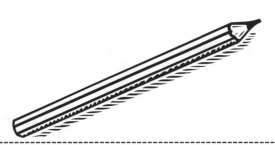

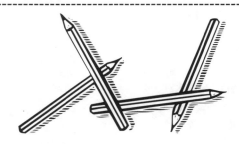

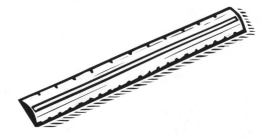

From *Imaginative Projects* by Matt Wicks © Cambridge University Press 2000 **PHOTOCOPIABLE**

Classroom language

2 Game play

Topic area
classroom language, games

Language focus
simple questions
instructions for games

Key vocabulary
board, dice, counter, roll, turn

Skills
speaking
writing

Level
pre-intermediate–
intermediate

Time
15–20 minutes

Materials
1 x page 16 per student

Before class
Photocopy page 16 for each student in your class.

In class

1 Write the following phrases on the board. These are the missing pieces of dialogue from *Playing by the rules* (page 16):

> Can I have the dice, please?
> It's your turn.
> What colour am I?
> Where do I start?
> What are the rules?
> How do I win?

2 Check that the students understand the meaning of all the sentences. Then ask them to work in pairs and put the sentences into the appropriate places in the comic strip on page 16.

3 Once the students have filled in the dialogue, get them to compare their answers with other students' answers. Finally, elicit the correct answers as a whole group.

> Answers
> 1 What are the rules?
> 2 How do I win?
> 3 Can I have the dice, please?
> 4 What colour am I?
> 5 Where do I start?
> 6 It's your turn.

Follow up

1 If students finish quickly, get them to write the phrases up on a poster so that it is always visible to the whole class.

2 In a future lesson, as revision, take the completed comic strip, with all the dialogue but without the letters a – o, cut it up and get the students to put the pictures back into the correct order.

15

PLAYING BY THE RULES

Fill in the missing words.

a *I want to play. Will you show me?*

b *No. It is too difficult for you.*

c *I need help to clean the kitchen.*

d *I have a good idea.*

e *OK dad. When we finish the game.*

f *The person who loses must help dad, OK?*

g 1 _____

h *It's easy. You roll the dice, then move your counter on the board.*

i 2 _____

j *The first person to finish wins. You can start.*

k *OK* 3 _____ *Yes, here you are.*

l 4 _____ *You are blue.*

m 5 _____ *You start here.*

n *OK* 6 _____

o ..... later *Are you coming to help me?* *Yes dad.*

From *Imaginative Projects* by Matt Wicks © Cambridge University Press 2000 **PHOTOCOPIABLE**

3 Speaking

Topic area
classroom language, people

Language focus
simple questions
will for predictions

Key vocabulary
questionnaire, role play, volunteer

Skills
speaking

Level
pre-intermediate–intermediate

Time
15 minutes

Materials
1 x page 18 per student

Before class
Photocopy page 18 for each student.

In class

1   Tell the students that they are going to think about how well they work together. Ask them to arrange themselves in a line starting with the people who think that they are 'good to work with' and going down to the people who think that they are 'not good to work with'. Once the line is complete (and there may be some debate about this), tell the class to remember where they were standing in the line, and then to return to their seats.

2   Put the students in pairs and ask them to look at the questionnaire.

3   They read through the questions and put the answers that they think their partner will give in the column that says *What you think your partner will answer*.

4   Once everybody has finished, the students then interview their partners and find out what they would really say, filling in the *What your partner answers* column on the questionnaire as they do so.

5   Now they have to give their partner a score using the chart below which can be written on the board or read out.

Scores		
1 (a) 0	(b) 10	(c) 0
2 (a) 10	(b) 5	(c) 0
3 (a) 0	(b) 2	(c) 10
4 (a) 7	(b) 10	(c) 0
5 (a) 2	(b) 5	(c) 10
6 (a) 10	(b) 0	(c) 0
7 (a) 7	(b) 10	(c) 0
8 (a) 5	(b) 0	(c) 10

6   Now tell the students what their scores mean.

> **50–80**   You are an excellent student and everybody will love working with you. In fact, you are so good – why not become a teacher?
>
> **25–50**   Sometimes you are a good student and sometimes you are a bad one. Some people will really like working with you and some people won't.
>
> **0–25**   You are a very lazy student. You do not work well with other people. You are the type of student who does something wrong and then laughs.

7   The pairs can now compare what they thought their partner would be like with what their partner is really like.

8   Once everybody has finished, the class can compare their results as a whole (in a fun way, not taking it too seriously) and see how close the ranking exercise (Step 1) was compared to the final results.

Questionnaire

1 You don't know your partner's name. Do you:
a invent a new name for them.
b ask him/her what their name is.
c not talk to them.

2 You disagree with your partner. Do you:
a say 'Sorry, I don't agree.'
b say 'No, that's wrong.'
c laugh.

3 You cannot understand your partner's pronunciation. Do you:
a ignore them.
b say 'Sorry?'
c say 'I'm sorry, could you repeat that, please?'

4 Your teacher tells you to choose characters in a role play. Do you:
a choose the one you want.
b ask everybody else what they want to do.
c refuse to do anything.

5 Your teacher tells you to make notes in your group. Do you say:
a 'You make notes.'
b 'I'll make notes.'
c 'Who wants to make notes?'

6 You don't understand what your teacher has told you to do. Do you:
a say 'Sorry, I don't understand.'
b let your partners do the work and pretend you understand.
c think about your girl/boy friend.

7 The teacher asks for a volunteer. Do you:
a always volunteer.
b sometimes volunteer.
c never volunteer.

8 You think that the activity you are doing is boring. Do you:
a do it quickly so that you can finish.
b not do it and think about your favourite pop star.
c tell the teacher that it is not interesting and ask if you can do something else.

● ●

ANSWERS:

What you think your partner will answer

1 . . . .
2 . . . .
3 . . . .
4 . . . .
5 . . . .
6 . . . .
7 . . . .
8 . . . .

What your partner answers

1 . . . .
2 . . . .
3 . . . .
4 . . . .
5 . . . .
6 . . . .
7 . . . .
8 . . . .

1 The island

LEVEL: Elementary–intermediate +

USING THIS PROJECT: This project is about islands. The parts of it can be done in any order, although they are presented here in a suggested logical order.

It begins with students inventing the world of their project by creating an island of their own (1.1), followed by a survival-type game (1.2). Students are then invited to imagine themselves really stranded with only a CD player for company (1.3), before studying the most famous castaway of all, Robinson Crusoe (1.4).

There are plenty of ways of extending this project: keeping 'castaway diaries' in which students record their (imagined) struggles to survive, making messages in bottles that they can send to other students / classes, or even setting up island communities with rules and structures that they have to persuade other students to obey.

In terms of timing, this project can be spread out over a long period of time as the links are primarily thematic and can, therefore, be integrated at appropriate points of a syllabus without relying on students having done the previous sections.

	1.1 Island poster	1.2 Travels with my rucksack	1.3 Desert island students	1.4 Robinson Crusoe
SKILLS	• speaking • writing	• speaking	• speaking	• speaking • reading • writing
TIME	60–90 minutes	45–60 minutes	30–40 minutes	45 minutes
PREPARATION	• finding magazine pictures • photocopying	• photocopying • producing an island map if 1.1 was not done	• photocopying • optional: finding popular songs	• photocopying • cutting up
CLASS SIZE	3 plus	6 plus	6 plus	any
PAGE NUMBER	20	22	24	26

1.1 Island poster

Topic area
travel, survival, maps

Language focus
descriptions
modals of ability
prepositions of position

Key vocabulary
geographical words
(*desert, jungle, wood, sea,
forest, stream, mountain,
plain, meadow, town, city,
village, ruins,* etc.)

Skills
speaking
writing

Level
elementary–
intermediate

Time
60–90 minutes

Materials
old magazines with lots
of pictures of places
1 x page 21 per 3
students
sheets of A3 card
scissors
pens
glue
(See page 13 for extra
activity on creating
things.)

Before class
1   Find old magazines with pictures of landscapes / seascapes that students can cut up.
2   Photocopy one page 21 for each group of three students in the class.

In class
1   Make sure that students know the language used in creating things (see page 13).
2   Brainstorm all of the types of terrain that the group can think of and write them on the board (pictures from magazines or maps can be used as prompts here). Useful words include: *desert, jungle, wood, sea, forest, stream, mountain, plain, meadow, town, city, village, ruins,* etc.
3   Get the students into groups of three and hand out copies of page 21 (one per group).
4   Tell the students to fill in the map with their own plan of the area, including different terrain types, etc. They should decide on specific icons to represent different terrain and complete the key with those icons. In addition, they can use terrain types that are not included in the key and add the symbols themselves in the blank space next to one of the = signs.
5   Now tell the students to paste their maps into the centre of a piece of A3 card.
6   Each group selects five areas of their map they feel are of special interest (e.g. some old ruins, a beautiful mountain range, a city, etc.). On a separate sheet of paper they write a short paragraph describing each area, as well as some information about what you can see and do there.
7   When the paragraphs are completed and checked, the students stick them around the map of the island and draw lines to connect the texts to the map.
8   Finally, to make the posters more attractive, the students choose pictures from magazines and glue these under (or above) each paragraph as illustrations of what can be seen at each place of interest.

Variation
The pictures can be found before the text is written to provide additional inspiration. It also allows more precise descriptions and vocabulary activation, although it can mean that students spend too long on the picture selection and not enough on the writing, so you should set a strict time limit.

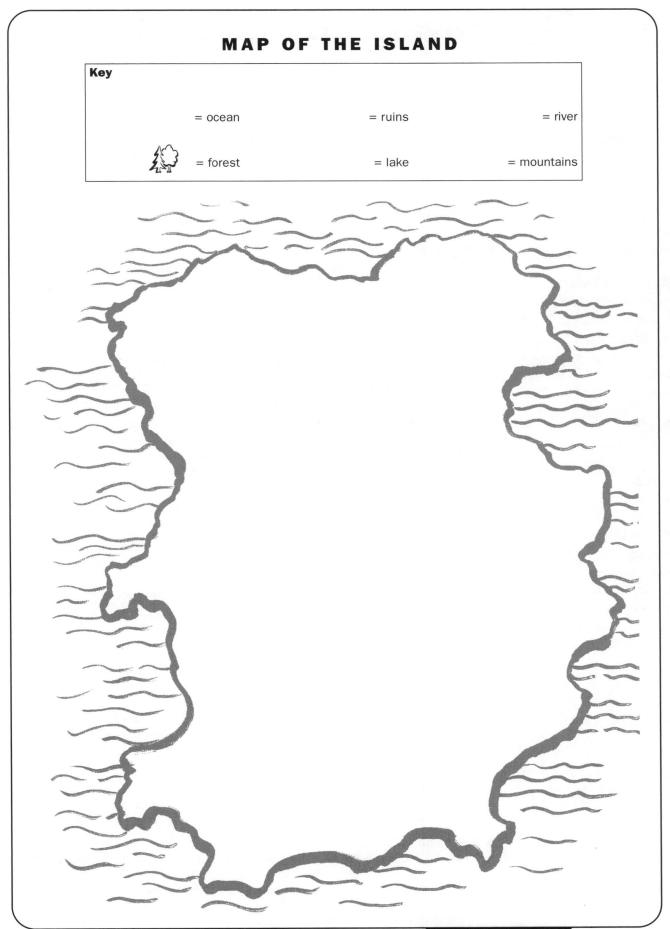

MAP OF THE ISLAND

Key

= ocean = ruins = river

= forest = lake = mountains

1.2 Travels with my rucksack

Topic area
travel, survival, desert islands

Language focus
conditionals
modals of possibility

Key vocabulary
rucksack, settlement
(some geographical words from 1.1)

Skills
speaking (See page 17.)

Level
intermediate +

Time
45–60 minutes

Materials
1 x page 23 per 4 students
1 x island map per 4 students

Before class

1 Photocopy page 23 once per four students in your class.

2 If students have not done 1.1, Island poster, you will need to draw a quick sketch map of an island for them using the outline on page 21. Photocopy this once per four students.

3 If students have done 1.1, Island poster, then choose one of their maps and photocopy it once per four students in your class.

In class

1 Make sure that students know language for speaking activities (see pages 17–18).

2 Explain to the students that they have won first prize in a school competition and are going to be sent on a round-the-world cruise.

3 Put them into groups of three or four and get them to imagine all of the things that they might see on the trip. Try to involve all the senses. Sitting on the deck, what do you hear? What can you smell? Does the air have any taste? etc.

4 Now put the students into different groups. Ask them to report to their new colleagues on what they discussed in Step 3.

5 Once everybody is comfortable, tell them that disaster has struck! There has been an explosion in the engine room and the ship is sinking. They can feel the heat of the flames and smell burning. (Alternatively, show them a clip of James Cameron's *Titanic* to get them in the mood.) There is only time for them to retrieve one rucksack's worth of supplies per group.

6 Give each group a copy of the Rucksack chart on page 23 and tell them that they have five minutes to fill it in with the things that they want to take with them.

7 Collect the completed Rucksack charts and then tell the students that the confusion is so great, with everybody trying to escape from the ship, that they accidentally pick up the wrong bag. Then, shuffle the Rucksack charts and hand them out again (making certain that no group receives their own back).

8 Fortunately, you can tell them, they are all strong swimmers and manage to make it to safety on a nearby island. Give each group a map of the island (see Before class Steps 2 and 3).

9 Each group is then given 15 minutes to deal with three basic problems:
(i) Where are they going to set up their base – and why?
(ii) What are they going to eat?
(iii) How are they going to defend themselves against predators?
Remember they can only use things that grow naturally or the supplies in their rucksacks. Write the three problems on the board or an OHT for the students to refer to.

10 The groups report back on what rucksack contents they ended up with and how they used the objects to solve their problems. Allow the other groups to challenge them if their solutions are not practical.

11 The groups then suggest ways in which they might be able to attract attention or build a ship to get off the island. This should be quite a brief part of the activity.

12 The students report back on their ideas for escape. You can decide the winner based on the best method of escape, or simply declare that any group with a reasonable escape plan manages to get away.

RUCKSACK CHART

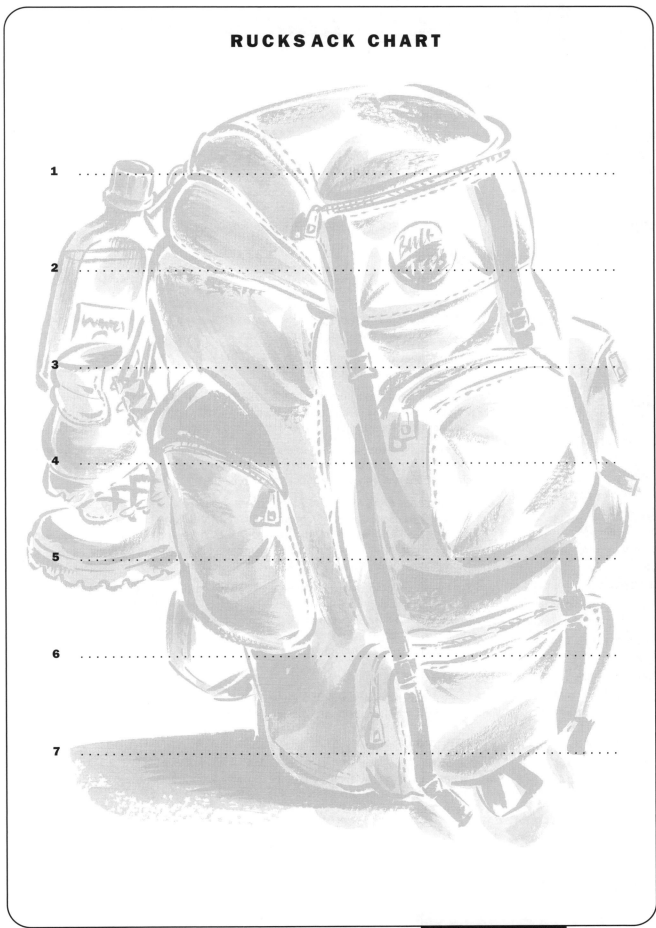

1 . . . .

2 . . . .

3 . . . .

4 . . . .

5 . . . .

6 . . . .

7 . . . .

1.3 # Desert island students

Topic area
travel, music, desert islands, food (see Variation)

Language focus
question forms
past verb forms

Key vocabulary
none

Skills
speaking (See page 17.)

Level
pre-intermediate–intermediate

Time
homework preparation: 30–40 minutes
if additional activities are used: up to 2 hours

Materials
1 x page 25 per student + 10 extra copies
optional: recordings of popular songs
optional: tape recorder and/or CD player
sheets of A4 paper

Before class

1   Photocopy one page 25 for each student and ten extra.

2   The day before you want the students to do this activity, give them a copy of the blank Top ten desert island songs sheet (page 25) and for homework ask them to fill it in with the name of their ten favourite songs and the artists who perform them.

3   Optional: Gather together a collection of currently popular songs (or ask the students to bring in a few of their favourites).

In class

1   Make sure that students know classroom language for speaking activities (see page 17).

2   Tell the students that they are going to be marooned on a desert island for six weeks. They are only allowed to take with them ten songs and one item of food.

3   In pairs, they have to compare their lists and then come up with a combined list of ten songs. Give them a limit of about ten minutes to do this.

4   When the pairs have completed this task, put them with another pair and get them to make a new list of ten songs. (They will have twenty to start with, but it is likely that some of these will be on both lists, and so this will not take very long.)

5   The process is repeated (i.e. each four combines with another four, then eights with eights, etc.) until the whole class is together, or, in the case of a very large class, there are only two groups.

6   The students are then put into ten groups (or fewer with small classes). Each group is given one song, which everybody in that group needs to know, so the groups should be based on that criterion. They must then decide what the song makes them think of – it may be a memory, a smell, an event, anything. If they cannot think of anything, they can invent something.

7   Each group should take an A4 piece of paper and record everybody's experiences in two or three sentences to make a 'Memory sheet' which can go on the wall next to the top ten songs as a part of the project. Meanwhile, play as many of the students' songs as possible (if you have brought them in, see Before class Step 3) to help create the atmosphere.

Variation
This activity can be done with food rather than music for younger students, or TV programmes if you have a class who are not particularly musical.

Follow up
Students can make their own version of *Desert Island Discs*, a British radio programme, in which the host interviews famous people about the eight CDs they would like to have when stranded on a desert island. The guest explains why the CDs are important. In class this can be done in groups, with a 'host' asking several other students about one CD each. Help groups prepare a suitable list of questions, and monitor answers, which need not be true. If possible, record the programme including the music as appropriate. This also ties in nicely with the Radio show (6, page 75).

what's your favourite song?

why do you like it?

who is it by?

TOP 10 DESERT ISLAND SONGS

1 ....
By ....
2 ....
By ....
3 ....
By ....
4 ....
By ....
5 ....
By ....
6 ....
By ....
7 ....
By ....
8 ....
By ....
9 ....
By ....
10 ....
By ....

1.4 Robinson Crusoe

Topic area
desert islands, survival, stories, famous people

Language focus
narrative tenses
articles
reference devices

Key vocabulary
mutineer, mutiny, pirate, shipwreck, castaway, native, cannibal, cave, fence, footprint, bones

Skills
speaking
reading
writing

Level
intermediate +

Time
45 minutes

Materials
1 x page 27 per 3 students
1x page 28 per 3 students
optional: class readers
optional: glue

Before class

1   Photocopy one page 27 per three students (or per pair if the class is small) and cut the cards up.

2   Photocopy one page 28 per three students (again, one per pair if the class is small).

In class

1   Ask the students what they know (if anything) about Robinson Crusoe. (He was the hero of a novel by Daniel Defoe written in the early 18th century. The story was inspired by the experience of Alexander Selkirk, a castaway from 1704–1709. Robinson Crusoe was on his island for nearly 30 years.)

2   Check that they understand the key words for this exercise. If necessary, use drawings or act out the words.

3   Divide the students into equal-sized groups and give each group a shuffled set of the cards on page 27 and the chronology chart on page 28. Their task is to put the cards in order. They should look at dates, tenses, and words such as *later*, *after that*. They stick or place cards on the correct square of the chronology chart, beginning in 1632 with the earliest card.

4   The groups compare notes and report back. Give the solution if there is disagreement.

> SOLUTION
> 1=E; 2=J; 3=H; 4=B; 5=M; 6=C; 7=L; 8=D; 9=F; 10=A; 11=G; 12=I; 13=K

This activity can be done as a stand-alone writing / grammar exercise to introduce or practise the use of reference devices.

Follow up

1   Students read a graded reader of *Robinson Crusoe* and write their own diary entry for the castaway.

2   (for an advanced group or a literature course) The story of Robinson Crusoe can be used as a basis of comparison with other castaway stories, such as Lucy Irvine's *Castaway* or William Golding's *Lord of the Flies*. One group can read each story and compare the way in which each survivor / group of survivors dealt with the problems of shelter, food and companionship. They can present their work orally or in writing.

3   (to encourage students to use graded readers) Each group reads another reader and makes a set of cards for that book, like the ones on page 27. They shuffle their cards and exchange sets with other groups who must arrange them correctly. This exercise has huge potential in that it really gets them to look at linkers and reference devices, but it needs very careful monitoring to make certain that the cards really can be sequenced.

ROBINSON CRUSOE CARDS

Cut the following cards out and shuffle them.

E
My name is Robinson Crusoe. I was born in 1632. My father did not want me to become a sailor, but I became one when I was 27.

D
A few months later, I saw another sign: a boat and some human bones. Cannibals had been on my island. I watched the sea every day for two or three months in case they returned.

J
We had been at sea for twelve days when there was a terrible storm and everybody else on the ship was killed.

F
Nothing happened until a few years later when I saw five boats of cannibals arriving with two prisoners ... ready to be eaten.

H
When I woke up, I was alone on a desert island. I found a cave to live in and cut down trees to make a home to protect myself.

A
I saved one of them. He started to learn English and I gave him a name: Friday.

B
Ten months later, I began to explore the island for the first time.

G
We lived together for many years after that. When I was 55, an English ship arrived at our island. However, there was a problem.

M
After looking around the island, I decided to make a boat – but, after four months' work, I discovered that I had built it too far from the sea. I felt stupid!

I
The captain had been taken prisoner by his crew.

C
I felt very unhappy because of my mistake.

K
We rescued him and helped him defeat the mutineers. He was very grateful and took us both back to England.

L
I had recovered from my disappointment when, one day, I saw a footprint in the sand. I was terrified by the idea that other people might be on my island. I made my fence much stronger.

ROBINSON CRUSOE CHRONOLOGY CHART

Put the cards in the correct place.

1 – 1632	**8**
2	**9**
3	**10**
4	**11**
5	**12**
6	**13 – 1687**
7	

2 Movie moguls

LEVEL: Intermediate–upper-intermediate

USING THIS PROJECT: This project introduces students to movies and performance through an audition (2.1). They then meet some of the vocabulary connected with movie (film) making in a game (2.2) and practise it by writing reviews (2.3). This vocabulary will be used in completing the largest part of the project in which they make their own film (2.4).

Before beginning this project, it may be necessary to tell the students what a *mogul* is. Try to create an image of a rich man or woman, with a gold watch, thick coat, wonderful car and demanding personality, who runs a film studio. Also explain that *movie* is another word for film, used more in the US than in Britain.

In addition, it should be noted that this project is best undertaken by a well-motivated group of students used to working autonomously. The last part of the project especially requires a considerable degree of responsibility and enthusiasm.

	2.1 The audition	**2.2** The mogul game	**2.3** Movie magazine	**2.4** Shooting
SKILLS	• speaking • pronunciation	• speaking	• speaking • writing • reading	• writing • speaking • reading
TIME	30 minutes	45 minutes	60 minutes	6–7 hours
PREPARATION	• photocopying • cutting • enlarging	• photocopying • cutting	• finding old movie magazines/pictures • photocopying • cutting	• arrange/borrow video camera and cassette • photocopying
CLASS SIZE	2 plus (ideally with 10)	4 plus	3 plus	6 plus (ideally with a larger class)
PAGE NUMBER	30	32	36	38

2.1 The audition

Topic area
media, people, drama

Language focus
adjectives and adverbs

Key vocabulary
adjectives: *happy, sad, angry, slow, quick, arrogant, romantic, terrifying* and the adverbs formed from these words

Skills
speaking
pronunciation

Level
intermediate +

Time
30 minutes

Materials
1 x cut up adjective pictures and adjective words on page 31 per pair
1 x text on page 31 per student
optional: tape recorder and cassette

Before class

1 Photocopy and cut up one set of adjective picture cards and one set of adjective word cards from page 31 per pair.

2 Photocopy (and possibly enlarge) one script from the audition section of page 31 per student.

In class

1 Put the students into pairs and give each pair a set of adjective cards. Don't let them look at the cards until you are ready.

2 When you say *'Go'* they have to try to match the adjective with the picture as quickly as possible. The first group to match all pictures and words correctly wins.

3 Now, get the class to make the adverbs which come from these adjectives. Demonstrate what you mean by writing *sad* and *sadly* on the board along with sample sentences (and ideally, pictures or mimes): *a sad man*, *a man walking sadly along a street.*

4 Students make the rest of the adjectives into adverbs and write them on a piece of paper.

5 Go around and help with the spelling where necessary (e.g. *happily* and *romantically*).

6 The first group to finish accurately (spellings included) wins.

7 Write a list of all the adverbs on the board. Check that students understand the meaning by miming actions in a particular manner (e.g. *sadly, happily*, etc.) and getting the students to call out the adverb that they think is appropriate.

8 Students work in pairs. Now write this sentence on the board: *You have the most beautiful eyes I have ever seen.* Each student says it to their partner in the manner of the various adverbs. Start with an easy one – romantically or happily – and then move on to the more difficult ones. Say it a few times for your students in each case so that they can mimic the intonation.

9 Tell the class that they are going to be auditioning for a part in the next big Hollywood movie.

10 Students work in pairs. Give each student a copy of the audition dialogue and give each person an adverb (a different one for A and B).

11 The pairs then go away and work on the dialogue, saying every line in the manner of the adverb.

12 Each pair comes back and presents the dialogue. Their classmates try to guess what the adverb was.

Variation

1 The students can choose their own adverbs to use in acting out the dialogue, not just words from Step 4.

2 For a shy class, record yourself and other members of staff doing the dialogue in various different ways. The students can then use the tape as listening practice to identify different adverbs.

ADJECTIVE CARDS: PICTURES

ADJECTIVE CARDS: WORDS

HAPPY	SAD	ANGRY	ROMANTIC
SLOW	QUICK	ARROGANT	TERRIFYING

THE AUDITION:

A: I look at you and I can only see happiness.
B: I look at you and I can only see sadness.
A: Oh dear!
B: I must tell you a secret.
A: Tell me! Tell me!
B: I love your brother/sister.
A: You cannot be serious! What about me?
B: I don't love you.
A: But why?
B: Because when I look at you I can only see sadness.
A: But when I look at you I can only see happiness.
B: I know!

The mogul game

Topic area
media, people, cinema, games

Language focus
media vocabulary
descriptions

Key vocabulary
camera, set, location, hit, blockbuster, producer, screening, director, wardrobe, cameraman, star, make-up, shoot, edit film types (e.g. *musical, action film,* etc.)
(See page 15 for extra activity on game play.)

Skills
speaking

Level
intermediate–
upper-intermediate

Time
45 minutes

Materials
1 x board on page 33 per 4 students
1 x cut up cards on page 34 per 4 students
3 x cut up cards on page 35 per 4 students
dice
scissors
counters

Before class

1 Photocopy one page 33 per four students (you may like to enlarge it, as well).

2 Photocopy and cut up one set of cards on page 34 per four students.

3 Photocopy and cut up three sets of cards on page 35 per four students.

In other words, for each group of four you should have one board (page 33), one set of mogul cards (page 34) and three sets of actor cards (page 35) – you can always get the students to cut up the actor cards themselves to save preparation time.

In class

1 Make sure all students are familiar with the classroom language connected with game play (see page 15).

2 Explain to the students that they are in charge of a big film studio, and they are very rich. They are, in fact, moguls. They now want to make a new film, but to do that they must get 25 actors.

3 Divide the class into small groups (about four per group) and give each group a copy of the board, one set of mogul cards and three sets of actor cards.

4 Shuffle the mogul cards and place them face down on each board in the MOGUL CARD box. Place the actor cards face up in the ACTOR CARD box.

5 Either explain the rules, or give each group a copy of the rules, below.

RULES
(i)   Each player throws the dice. The player with the highest number starts.
(ii) Each player takes five actors from the ACTOR CARD box to begin with.
(iii) Each player puts their counter on the square that says START HERE and throws the dice. Move the number of spaces on the dice.
(iv) If you land on a square that says MOGUL CARD, then take one of the mogul cards. You must answer the question or follow the instructions on the card. Check the answer with the other people in your group. If you do not all agree then check with your teacher. If you got the answer right, you can take one actor from the actor pile. If you got the answer wrong, you have to put an actor back into the pile.
(v)   When you have finished with the mogul card, put it back at the bottom of the pack.
(vi) The winner is the first mogul to get 25 actors.

MOGUL CARD ANSWERS
BLOCKBUSTER: (b); HIT: (b); PRODUCER: (a); SCREENING: (a); the person who films a movie is called the CAMERAMAN/WOMAN; the person who tells actors what to do is called the DIRECTOR; the place where actors get their clothes is called the WARDROBE DEPARTMENT; very famous actors are called STARS; the actors are Brad Pitt; Julia Roberts; Arnold Schwarzenegger; Whoopi Goldberg; a MAKE-UP PERSON puts on all the actors' lipstick, face-paint, etc.; a SPECIAL EFFECTS PERSON makes all the explosions, spaceships, etc. in a film; TO SHOOT A MOVIE = to film a movie; TO EDIT = to cut the film up and put it back into the correct order.

MOGUL GAME BOARD

THE MOGUL GAME

THERE IS AN EARTHQUAKE AND YOUR STUDIO IS DAMAGED. LOSE FIVE ACTORS.

REVIEW TIME! TELL THE REST OF YOUR CLASS ABOUT YOUR FAVOURITE FILM FOR ONE MINUTE AND GET TWO ACTORS.

MOGUL CARD

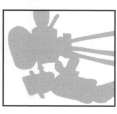

EVERYBODY HATES YOUR NEW FILM. NAME THREE SCIENCE FICTION FILMS OR LOSE AN ACTOR AND MISS A TURN.

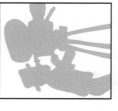

YOU ENTER A MOVIE CONTEST. NAME TEN ENGLISH LANGUAGE FILMS IN TWO MINUTES AND WIN THREE ACTORS.

THE ACTORS WANT MORE MONEY. NAME THREE MUSICALS OR MISS A TURN.

ACTOR CARD

MOGUL CARD

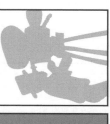

YOU HAVE A GOOD AUDITION. GET TWO ACTORS TO WORK FOR YOU.

MOGUL CARD

YOUR STUDIO BUILDS A NEW SET. YOU GET ANOTHER ACTOR FOR YOUR MOVIE.

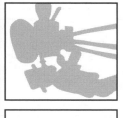

YOUR STAR LEAVES YOUR MOVIE BECAUSE YOU ARE NOT PAYING HER ENOUGH. NAME THREE ACTION FILMS OR MISS A TURN.

YOU MAKE A MOVIE AND GET THREE ACTORS FOR YOUR NEXT FILM.

THE DIRECTOR LEAVES YOUR FILM TO WORK FOR ANOTHER STUDIO. NAME THREE ROMANTIC FILMS OR GO BACK FOUR SPACES.

MOGUL CARD

START HERE

MOGUL CARDS

A BLOCKBUSTER is (a) a bad film (b) a very successful film or (c) an important actor.	A HIT (in the film world) is (a) something painful (b) a successful film (c) an unsuccessful film.	A PRODUCER is the person who (a) controls all the finances of the film or (b) tells actors what to do.	A SCREENING is (a) a special showing of the movie (b) part of a cinema or (c) the actors' seats.
Hollywood calls. Take one actor.	Hollywood calls. Take one actor.	Hollywood calls. Take one actor.	Hollywood calls. Take one actor.
The person who films a movie is called the _____.	The person who tells the actors what to do is called the _____.	The place where actors get their clothes is called the _____.	Very famous actors are called _____.
Tell us four things that you would find in a cinema and what you do with them.	Talk about the worst film you have ever seen for one minute.	Do you prefer to watch movies on TV or at the cinema? Tell us why.	Would you like to be a famous actor/actress? Tell us why/why not.
Who is this actor?	Name two movies this actress has been in.	Name two movies this actor has been in.	Who is this actress?
What does a MAKE-UP PERSON do?	What does a SPECIAL EFFECTS PERSON do?	What does the phrase TO SHOOT A MOVIE mean?	What does the verb TO EDIT mean, in films?
Give three reasons why you like your favourite film.	Name three types of film (e.g. science fiction).	Tell the group who your favourite actor/actress is and why.	What was the last film that you saw? Tell us three things you liked or disliked about it.
Name three films made in your country.	Every year actors get a special award called an Oscar. Who would you give an Oscar to, and why?	Tell the group two reasons why you like/don't like westerns.	Tell the group two reasons why you like/don't like science fiction movies.
Draw a picture on the board of a film you like – without speaking! The rest of the group must guess the name of the film. If they can't, you must miss a turn.	Draw a picture on the board of a film you like – without speaking! The rest of the group must guess the name of the film. If they can't, you must miss a turn.	Mime the title of a film you like – without speaking. The rest of the group must guess the name of the film. If they can't, you must miss a turn.	Mime the title of a film you like – without speaking. The rest of the group must guess the name of the film. If they can't, you must miss a turn.

ACTOR CARDS

2.3 Movie magazine

Topic area
media, people, newspapers

Language focus
reported speech
adjectives (*wonderful, terrible*, etc.)
superlatives (see follow-up activity)

Key vocabulary
blockbuster, hit, producer, screening, director, wardrobe, stars, make-up, special effects, to shoot, to edit, science fiction, action, Oscar (see 2.2)
also *review, reviewer, plot, location*

Skills
speaking (See page 17.)
writing
reading

Level
intermediate +

Time
60 minutes

Materials
I x cut up review cards on page 37 per 3 students
I x cut up suggestions card on page 37 per pair
scissors glue A3 paper old magazines with pictures of movie stars

Before class

1 Collect some old magazines with pictures of famous movie stars and/or scenes from movies that are currently popular.

2 Photocopy and cut up one set of review cards on page 37 per three students.

3 Photocopy the suggestions card from page 37 for each pair in your class.

In class

1 Make sure students know language for speaking activities (see page 17).

2 Divide the class into groups of three (or pairs, in smaller classes).

3 Give each student one of the review cards that you have cut up from page 37. Tell them to read it but not to show it to their partner. Tell them that they need to remember as much as possible about their card.

4 Once each student has finished, collect in the review cards and get them to summarise the review that they read in their own words to their partners.

5 Next read out the five numbered questions from page 37. Each group starts with three points. After each question, any student who knows the answer stands up. Choose the quickest. If the answer is right, their group gets a point. If it is wrong, they lose one. The group whose representative stood up second may then try to answer the question. The group with the most points wins.

6 Now tell the students that they are going to write reviews of their favourite films for a magazine. In a large class, it is better to produce two or even three magazines with half (or a third) of the class working on each one.

7 Divide the class into pairs and give each pair a copy of the suggestions card. Brainstorm (as a class) all the recent films that they have seen at the cinema, on TV or on video. Write about 20 names on the board.

8 Each pair then chooses a film they have both seen and writes a review of it using the review cards as models and the questions on the suggestions card as prompts.

9 The first pair to finish can then start compiling a film magazine. They take a sheet of A3 paper (or more than one in a large group) and fold it in half to form an A4 magazine. Then they stick the reviews onto the paper, leaving a space next to each review for a picture. The pairs who finish second and third can join in. Students may word process their reviews and the editors cut and paste them using a computer.

10 Each group then looks through the movie magazines and selects an appropriate picture to put next to their review.

11 The rest of the class look through their magazines and select a picture they like. These are all put together and cut and pasted to form a collage for the cover.

12 Photocopy the magazine for each student and put one copy up on the wall.

Follow up

You can extend this activity by having a centre spread 'Interview with a Star' in which students write an interview with a famous actor/actress. (See 6.1 for advice on this.) The magazine could also include a 'Class Oscars' section in which the class lists prizes for their own 'Best Actress', etc., to practise superlatives.

TITANIC

Titanic is a famous film because of its stars, Leonardo DiCaprio and Kate Winslet and its director, James Cameron.

Although it won many Oscars in 1998, I was very disappointed by the film. It was shot very well by Cameron, and the special effects were spectacular, but the story was very poor. The plot quickly became repetitive with diCaprio and Winslet running up and down corridors again and again and again.

However, I did like the music (by James Horner) and thought that the wardrobe department created some wonderful costumes.

RATING: ✷✷

STAR WARS I: The Phantom Menace

This is a great science fiction film, and will definitely be a hit for writer/director George Lucas.

The acting is superb, especially young Jake Lloyd as Anakin and Ewan MacGregor as Obi-Wan Kenobi. This is a film that is well-known for its special effects and, although they were very good, I found them a little bit disappointing, especially in the big fight scene.

However, the make-up was excellent! I really believed that there were aliens living on other planets.

(And I loved Jar-Jar Binks, what a funny creature!)

RATING: ✷✷✷✷

JAMES BOND: The World is Not Enough

This is a very exciting film, from the first moments in the helicopter to the final peaceful moments on the beach. Pierce Brosnan (as Bond for the third time) is wonderful, and Robert Carlyle plays a tremendous villain – Renard.

Like all Bond films, there is lots of running around exotic locations (Bilbao) and more familiar ones (the Millennium Dome). Although the story is very simple, the action and special effects are exciting. It will certainly be a hit this summer, possibly even the biggest Bond block-buster ever.

The film has been shot wonderfully and edited together so that every scene is very short and very entertaining. What a great movie! Go and see it!

RATING: ✷✷✷✷✷

SUGGESTIONS CARD

Some questions to help you write your reviews

Which actors/actresses did you like?
Why/why not?
Did you think the movie had a good story?
What about the wardrobe, make-up and special effects – were they good?
Were there many locations?
Do you think it will be a hit or not?

QUESTIONS

1   Which film did the reviewer like the music in?
2   Which film was shot near the sea?
3   Which film ended with a big fight?
4   Which two films did the reviewers really like?
5   Which two films featured a lot of running about?

ANSWERS

1   *Titanic*
2   *James Bond*
3   *Star Wars*
4   *Star Wars* and *James Bond*
5   *Titanic* and *James Bond*

2.4 Shooting

Topic areas
media, crime, cinema, drama

Language focus
instructions
direct speech

Key vocabulary
camera, scene, location, zoom, action, cut
if doing the version on page 40: *judge, victim, morgue, prosecution, defence, lawyer, repair*

Skills
writing
speaking
reading

Level
intermediate–upper-intermediate (but can be adapted to any level)

Time
Lesson 1 90 minutes
Lesson 2 60–90 minutes
Lesson 3 60 minutes
Lesson 4 approx. 2 hours
Lesson 5 30–50 minutes

A note on timing
The times given are very approximate, because time needed will depend on the number of students you have and how able they are to work unsupervised. In addition, technical matters, such as teaching the students to use the camera, can take a variable amount of time. If you are working in England you will also need to make allowances for the weather!

Before class

1 Find a video camera and make sure you know how it works. Also reserve it in advance for the lessons required.

2 Photocopy and cut up one set of character cards on page 40 per group. Each group can consist of as many students as you like, but twelve is a good maximum.

3 Photocopy one story card on page 40 for each group.

In class

1 *Lesson 1*
   The characters: Explain to the students that they are going to make a movie and then ask for volunteers to be actors. They decide if they want big, small or walk-on parts (but these will be given other jobs too).

2 The people who do not want to act are given other roles – one of them will be the director, one the wardrobe person, one (or more) the cameraman/woman and, if necessary, one will be in charge of props.

3 The actors choose the characters that they are going to play. This can be done in one of two ways, either by using the **character cards** on photocopiable page 40, or – in more self-motivated groups – by the group choosing appropriate characters. (*He is the murderer, She can be the evil scientist,* etc.) The **character cards** are meant as introductions only. Get the students to fill in the gaps.

4 Students fill in the names on their character cards. Then give them time to 'flesh out' their character by making notes about his/her life, occupation, relationships, etc., and telling their partner about it.

5 *The story:* The students construct the story. This can also be done in two ways:
   (a) The students brainstorm a series of events and coincidences (e.g. a murder, the victim knew the murderer's wife; they went to school together). Write all of these on the board until there are enough ideas. The group then leaves out the ideas that don't work, until there is a list of about seven or eight good ideas. These are then put into sequence and connected. Help them with linking words, such as *then, meanwhile, however*. At this stage they may drop or modify some ideas.
   (b) Use the story idea from photocopiable page 40.
   Note If you choose this method, miss out Steps 6 and 7.

6 Once the students have the ideas, they work in small groups to write a one-page summary from the notes on the board.

7 The best summary is then chosen (by you) for the film.

8 *Scene breakdown:* Divide the class up into four or five groups. They read the summary of the plot and agree together where the scene breaks occur. This is essentially getting them to think about where logical or paragraph breaks might occur, and can be set for homework.

2.4 **Shooting** (continued)

Materials

1 x cut up character
cards on page 40 per
group
1 x story card on page
40 per student
video camera
video cassette
TV

9 *Lesson 2*
Having agreed the places where scene breaks occur, now assign a particular scene to each group. The students are going to write the script of the scene you have allocated them.

10 The writing stage requires a high degree of organisation as things which happen in the first scene will affect later scenes. One student in each group should be nominated as the researcher, regularly checking the other groups' work to find out the latest information and to check that all the stories fit together. The story may be modified as they work. However, it is wise to keep to a strict time limit and make certain that students keep more or less to the prepared storyline.

11 *Between Lessons 2 and 3*
Photocopy the script for everyone.

12 *Lesson 3*
Once the script is ready, checked and photocopied, the actors can begin working on rehearsals. The director should help organise this. You should work with students on pronunciation and intonation.

13 Meanwhile, the students with smaller parts can prepare the props – find them, draw anything necessary for the set, search for locations, etc.

14 *Lesson 4* (and possibly *5* as well)
Go out and film the whole thing. One person should act as cameraperson in each scene. Give people with smaller parts the opportunity, and let more than one have a go. Always remember the key things are the pronunciation, the clarity of speech and the fun. If the film doesn't look like a great Hollywood blockbuster, it really doesn't matter.

15 Before watching the video (Step 16) you may try putting some of the mistakes together as a grammar auction. (In a grammar auction you choose a collection of ten sentences, some correct, some not. The students each have £5,000 and they have to 'bid' for the correct sentences only. The group with the most correct sentences at the end of the game wins. The class then goes through the incorrect sentences and corrects them.)

16 *Lesson 5*
The students watch the video and make comments.

Follow up

1 Give some pronunciation correction using the video to show the errors they made. Be careful to comment as well on how good their performances were. (Being videoed in a foreign language is very challenging.)

2 Write a critical review of the film for a film magazine (see 2.3).

3 A strong group could write the 'novel' adaptation. For this activity, students brainstorm the difference between film and book (such as the depth of character and the fact that you see inside the characters' minds) and then each group writes a chapter (possibly on the computer if you have one) trying to concentrate on internal thoughts / descriptions, etc.

CHARACTER CARDS

You are _____, the bike repair man. You have a bicycle shop in _____ street.	You are _____, the assistant in the bike repair shop. You are not very clever.	You are _____, an old woman who lives near the bike repair shop.	You are _____, the very fashionable son/daughter of the old woman.
You are _____, the Detective Inspector of the local police.	You are _____, a policeman who hates her/his boss, the Detective Inspector.	You are _____, the victim	You are _____, you work in the morgue.
You are _____, the judge.	You are _____, the defence lawyer.	You are _____, the prosecution lawyer.	You are _____, the executioner.

STORY CARD

One day the bike repair man is repairing a bike for the old woman. Suddenly, the victim appears and starts to talk loudly to the bike repair man about some secret business arrangement. The bike repair man and the victim go outside to talk. The assistant to the bike repair man repairs the bike and gives it to the old woman and her fashionable son/daughter. They are leaving when they hear a strange sound, but when they search they find nothing. The bike repair man returns and says that he is going to lunch. The assistant investigates the back room of the shop and finds the dead body of the victim. He calls the police. The Inspector and his assistant arrive and they start to question everybody. First of all, they ask the bike repair man what happened, but he says that he doesn't know anything. Then, they speak to the old woman and the son/daughter, and they tell him about the strange sound. They go to the morgue and speak to the mortician who tells them that the victim was strangled – and he has found a fingerprint on the dead person's neck! The Inspector takes a copy of the fingerprint and goes to a local pub, where he meets the bike repair man. He buys the repair man a drink. The repair man drinks and leaves. When he has gone, the Inspector looks at the glass and sees that there is a fingerprint on it. He compares the fingerprint with the one that the mortician gave him – they are the same! The criminal is arrested in a struggle. Next day, in court, the judge listens to the defence and prosecution cases. (The lawyers interview the witnesses again.) Finally, the jury give their verdict: the bike repair man is guilty. He is executed.

3 Space City

LEVEL: Pre-intermediate–intermediate

USING THIS PROJECT: This is a narrative project and the story begins with the foundation of Space City (3.2), followed by the students travelling into space (3.3). Then, they meet hostile aliens and they have to defeat them (3.4).

In order to get students involved in the story, it is important to do the project over a short period of time and to have a designated area of the room to display the students' cities. Get them to imagine what jobs they might do, or where they might live, for example.

At the beginning of each part of the project explain to the students how what they are doing links in to the previous part, e.g. (for 3.2): 'Yesterday, we built Space City. Now, the problem is getting there – how do you imagine people travel to Space City?' This is followed by brainstorming their ideas. Then, explain that they are the travel agents organising space trips.

In addition, to build up a story, you can ask the students to write up an account every day of what happened to them in Space City: the first day would be a description of the city, the second might talk about the journey, the third about initial impressions of the aliens and the final day about the battle against them.

	3.1 Building the future	**3.2** The city of the future	**3.3** Travel to Space City	**3.4** Loving the alien
SKILLS	• speaking	• speaking • reading • writing	• speaking • reading • (optional: writing)	• speaking • pronunciation
TIME	20–35 minutes	100 minutes	50 minutes	40 minutes
PREPARATION	• photocopying • cutting	• photocopying • folding • finding glue, scissors, etc.	• photocopying • cutting • folding	• photocopying • cutting • (optional: making question cards)
CLASS SIZE	6 plus	6 plus	8 plus	6 plus
PAGE NUMBER	42	44	48	52

3.1 Building the future

Topic area
cities, buildings, the future

Language focus
comparatives
will for prediction

Key vocabulary
castle, palace, skyscraper, block of flats, house, temple, cottage, windmill, mosque, pyramid, church, tower

Skills
speaking

Level
pre-intermediate–intermediate

Time
20–35 minutes

Materials
1 x enlarged building pictures from page 43
1 cut up set of name cards from page 43 per 4 students
optional: picture dictionary

Before class

1   Photocopy and enlarge (if possible) one set of pictures from page 43. Stick them around the classroom wall.
Note If you have a large class you will have to put up more than one copy of each picture.

2   Photocopy and cut up one set of the name cards on page 43 per four students.

In class

1   Put the students in groups of four and give each group a copy of the name cards from page 43. They then have to move around the room sticking the correct word to each building (using blutak). Thus, for example, picture 1 would have *castle* attached to it. Alternatively, students could use this as a picture dictionary activity, in which they use their picture dictionaries to find the word and then write it on a piece of card and stick it to the picture on the wall.

2   When they have finished, move the pictures onto the board and ask the class to help you display them roughly in the order in which they were built. Students say which they think comes next, so that they are recalling the building vocabulary. There is no fixed order, and so the aim of the exercise is vocabulary revision rather than rigid historical accuracy, and it is left to you to decide which sequence works best, although it probably begins with the pyramids and ends with the skyscraper.

3   Ask each group to make up five or six sentences comparing various pictures with each other. Thus, *'The skyscraper is bigger than the cottage'*, *'More people live in a castle than in a cottage'*, etc.

4   Ask the students to predict what they think the buildings of the future will look like and what they will contain. Give them a specific date (two hundred years in the future, for example) and encourage them to be as inventive as possible. (They should think of the smells, colours and sounds that will be there, too.) They can either do this orally or they can draw their vision of the future (although they should not spend too long drawing, especially if you are going on to do the 'Space City map', 3.2 page 44).

5   As a final feedback stage, ask the students to tell or show the rest of the class the sort of things they have thought of. Finish by asking if they would like to live in this sort of a city themselves. Elicit the possible advantages and disadvantages.

BUILDING PICTURES

NAME CARDS

CASTLE	PALACE	SKYSCRAPER	BLOCK OF FLATS
HOUSE	TEMPLE	COTTAGE	WINDMILL
MOSQUE	PYRAMID	CHURCH	TOWER

3.2 The city of the future

Topic area
the future, cities, geography, art

Language focus
past tenses
will for prediction
descriptions

Key vocabulary
building vocabulary (see 3.1) *fur, crater, tablet, space suit, zoo, zero gravity, atmosphere, striker, goalkeeper*

Skills
reading
speaking
writing

Level
pre-intermediate–intermediate

Time
reading: 40 minutes
poster: approx. 60 minutes

Materials
1 x page 45 enlarged and cut up
1 x page 46 and 47 per student
glue
card for displays
scissors
coloured pens
(See page 13 for extra activity on creating things.)

Before class

1 Photocopy, enlarge and cut up one set of the questions on page 45.

2 Photocopy one each of pages 46 and 47 per student. These pages can either be copied back-to-back or glued together and folded along the 'fold here' lines to make authentic looking brochures.

In class

1 Hand out folded copies of the Space City brochure (pages 46 and 47). Give the students a few minutes to look at it and then ask them the questions on page 45. This can be done as a reading race. One student from each group runs to the teacher, collects a question (from page 45) on a strip of paper, and runs back to their group who write down the answer. The runners then take back the question and get another one. The winning group finishes first with the most correct answers.

2 Make sure that students are familiar with the language connected with creating things in the classroom (see page 13).

3 Tell the students that after replying to the advert in the brochure, they have been hired by Dr Deerson to make a display about Space City, man's greatest achievement.

4 Students brainstorm places that might be in Space City, in addition to those in the brochure (e.g. zero gravity swimming pool, space library, lunar zoo, hover train driving school, star disco, etc.). They then add the places mentioned in the text to their list.

5 Next the students begin designing their display. Each group presents it on coloured card. On the card they draw pictures of the imaginary places, while other members of the group write a short text under each one. They change roles regularly so that everybody does at least some writing. It is often easier if the text is written on paper, checked and then glued onto the master display afterwards.

6 Once completed the card is mounted on the wall and the students can show the other groups around their version of the city.

Variation

For older groups, this approach might not be suitable. They can design a map of the city instead, showing all the major roadways, spaceports, etc. If one group does the eastern side, one the western, etc., all the parts can be stuck together to make one large wall map of the whole city. Students can write and attach paragraphs about features of interest.

BROCHURE QUESTIONS

1 What did Dr Deerson do?

2 Look at the picture under the paragraph 'Why is it so popular?'
What do you think this picture is of? Why?

3 What happened to Miguel Kickaballabout?

4 When was Space City opened?

5 What problem did John, John and John solve? How?

6 Look at these sentences and correct any mistakes:

a Space City has been open for more than ten years.

b There are more visitors to Disneyworld than to Space City.

c Mario Marisco was the champion striker last year.

d Mario jumped so high that he left the atmosphere and hasn't returned since that day.

7 In the brochure it says that Dr Deerson 'has overseen' the whole project and that John, John and John 'overcame' the atmosphere problem. What do you think those words mean?

From *Imaginative Projects* by Matt Wicks © Cambridge University Press 2000 **PHOTOCOPIABLE**

Answers:
1 He had the idea for Space City.
2 A Lua Lua because it is a 'small furry animal'.
3 He jumped so high he went into orbit.
4 2065.
5 That there was no oxygen. They invented a special tablet.
6 a Space City has been open for ten years.
    b There are more visitors to Space City than to Disneyworld.
    c Mario Marisco was the champion goalkeeper this year.
    d Miguel jumped, not Mario.
7 'oversee' = supervise; 'overcome' = solve

WELCOME TO SPACE CITY 2075

fold here

URGENT! HELP REQUIRED

Dr Deerson will give one million universal credits to whoever designs the best map of Space City. It must be useful for tourists and you can include as many places as you can think of. Don't forget the Lua Lua restaurants.

REMEMBER 1,000,000 credits!

Mars Conglomerate
623 Olympus Mountain
http:// www.marsco.com

fold here

LUNAR FOOTBALL

On Friday afternoons in Space City, everybody from the President of the Moon to the smallest child stops work and goes outside the city to play Lunar Football. 'It's wonderful!' said Mario Marisco, this year's champion goalkeeper. 'Anybody can play and it's more fun than playing on Earth.'

Lunar football is different from Earth football because of the very low gravity. This means that the ball just floats through the air, sometimes as high as four kilometres! You have to be careful, though – last year Miguel Kickaballabout (the goalkeeper for Mars FC) jumped so high that he left the ground and disappeared into space!

WELCOME TO SPACE CITY BROCHURE FOR SUMMER 2075

The beginning

The project itself was the idea of one man: Dr Hoffmann Reinhold Deerson, and he has overseen every part of the construction. At first, there were some problems because, as you know, the Moon doesn't have an atmosphere – the builders couldn't breathe!

A clever solution

'That was a big problem,' Dr Deerson explains, 'but we have overcome all our difficulties. My colleagues John, John and John have developed special tablets which let people breathe even when there is no oxygen.'

So – what do people do?

During the day in Space City most people do the same jobs as you or I do on Earth. They work in the Space bank, in the government, the shops (selling space suits, for example). Children go to school and learn English and astronomy. But, Fridays are different . . .

- fold here

'IT WAS INCREDIBLE. I HAVE NEVER BEEN ANYWHERE IN THE UNIVERSE THAT HAS AS MANY WONDERFUL ATTRACTIONS AS SPACE CITY . . .'

Simon Regan, Chief Accountant, Space City

Space City

Space City was opened on the Moon ten years ago. Since then, more than twenty thousand people have moved here. However, it is not only people living here who fill the streets, but tourists as well. Nowadays, it is more popular than 'Disneyworld' in Florida or 'Queenworld' in London.

Why is it so popular?

Well, perhaps it is because it has got everything for the modern family: twenty-three cinemas (although not all of them have opened yet), a trip around the Moon every day in a rocket and, of course, many restaurants specialising in Lua Lua, small furry animals found only on the Moon's dark side in big craters.

- fold here

SPACE CITY

Our space is your space.

Topic area
travel, the future, drama

Language focus
numbers
money
question forms

Key vocabulary
names of the planets and objects in the solar system; *cabin, canal, dust, surface, hunting, surf, surfboard, compulsory, cruise, bankrupt*

Skills
speaking (See page 17 for extra activity.)
reading
writing if variation is done

Level
pre-intermediate+

Time
50 minutes

Materials
1x page 49 per 3 students
1x page 50 per 3 students
1x page 51 cut up

3.3 Travel to Space City

Before class

1 Photocopy and fold one page 49 per three students.

2 Photocopy and fold one page 50 per three students.

3 Photocopy and cut up one page 51.

4 You may rearrange the classroom into three distinct areas for the shops and the clients.

In class

1 Make sure that students are familiar with language connected with speaking activities (see page 17).

2 Divide the class into three groups: A Starr's Star Shuttles, B Tony's Time Trekkers, and C the rest of the class who are customers looking for holidays.

3 Group A reads page 49 and B reads page 50 (their respective holiday brochures).

4 Students in Group C receive the role cards from page 50. They are going on holiday with a partner and the role cards are subdivided into pairs. Set 6 (6A, 6B and 6C) are for the problem of odd-numbered classes. If you have an even number in your class, use cards 6A and 6B. If you have an odd number, then use 6C as well.

5 Group C prepares the questions they will ask the travel agents, the information they will need from them and how much they are willing or able to spend on their holidays (based on the information on their cards). Monitor their decisions.

6 The role play then begins with each travel agent trying to sell as many holidays as possible while the customers try to get the best bargain.

7 Each group visits a different travel agent as soon as they are free (you may need to limit the amount of time any group can spend with the travel agent, or, in a larger class, to separate the travel agents so that, for example, each member of Starr's Star Shuttles is dealing with a different set of customers).

8 Each group of holiday seekers must visit both travel agents at least once, but can revisit them if they need to.

9 The travel agents are allowed to make discounts. However, the maximum amount they are allowed to discount is 10%. It should be made clear to them, as well, that their aim is to make as much money as possible. Big discounts = small profits!

10 In the end, each group of customers announces and justifies their decision about their holiday destination. Make certain that they explain all the offers they were given and what it was that made them choose – the price? The service? The dates?

11 The travel agents report back on how much money they made. You can then tell the students which of the companies made a profit and which went bankrupt.

Variation

Students can make their own brochure up with their own planets and destinations (including Space City), which gives this activity a writing element as well.

Follow up

1 Students can do a follow-up activity in which they visit the travel agents again, this time as themselves, with their own reasons for a space age holiday.

2 Students can be sent out to the local travel agents to see how they compare with one another. (It is always a good idea to check with the travel agent before sending a group of students, though.)

STARR'S STAR SHUTTLES

MARS THE RED PLANET!

Three weeks in the luxurious Olympus Hotel with a zero gravity swimming pool and all-night parties in the famous Mars Bar!

The Pioneer VI Shuttles leave from Earth every Tuesday at 07.25 and most Fridays at 14.45, taking just over 23 hours to reach Clinton Spaceport on Mars.

Special excursions include trips to see where the first man landed on Mars' surface in 2004 and a tour of the dust canals.

THE RED PLANET!

COSTS AND DATES

DATE	Shuttle	Accommodation [2]	Excursions	Notes
	Cost [1]			
1 Jan–31 March	Cr1250	Cr920	Cr120 each	
1 April–31 Aug	Cr1980	Cr1010	Cr100 each	Dust canal tour unavailable
1 Sept–31 Dec	Cr1700	Cr960	Cr120 each	

[1] All prices are given in Universal Credits.
[2] Prices are based on a family of four. If there are more people, Cr100 is charged per person per week.

----------------------------- fold here

STARR'S STAR SHUTTLES

COMET CRUISE

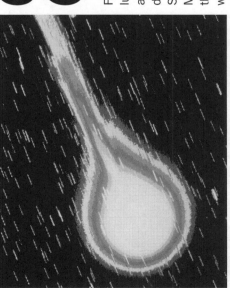

Fly with us on the luxurious Bopp Shuttle and you will spend ten days travelling the Solar System, seeing Venus, Mars, Space City and then on your last day we will take you close up to the famous Olla Poola Comet!

The Bopp Shuttle departs from Paris every Sunday morning at 10.00 and from Montreal every other day at 19.30.

Remember – everybody has their own luxury cabin during our cruise.

SEE A COMET!

COSTS AND DATES

DATE	Basic Cost [1]	Extra night in Space City	Extra night on Mars	Photos of the Comet [2]
1 Jan–31 March	Cr2250	Cr120	Cr100	Cr20 each
1 April–31 Aug	Cr3480	Cr220	Cr100 each	Cr20 each
1 Sept–31 Dec	Cr2890	Cr180	Cr100 each	Cr20 each

[1] All prices are given in Universal Credits.
[2] Photographs are genuine and signed by our official photographer.

TONY'S TIME TREKKERS

VENUS THE LOVE PLANET!

Spend six weeks in our romantic Venusian holiday village – it's fully heated!!

You can go sailing on the Ice Lake at weekends and go space suit skiing every day.

You and your family can get rich on Venus, too: our most popular excursion is diamond hunting in the fabulous Ice Mines.

The Flasher VI leaves from Siberia every day at 10.00 am and only takes 19 hours to reach Venus Central. WOW!

THE LOVE PLANET!

COSTS AND DATES

DATE	Shuttle Cost[1]	Accommodation[2]	Excursions	Notes
1 Jan–31 March	Cr1050	Cr1620	Cr420 each	
1 April–31 Aug	Cr1280	Cr1910	Cr300 each	Book early for diamond hunting.
1 Sept–31 Dec	Cr1950	Cr1860	Cr420 each	No skiing in December

[1] All prices are given in Universal Credits.
[2] Prices are based on two people. If more than two people want to go, each person must pay Cr200 extra per week.

fold here

TONY'S TIME TREKKERS

SURF THE BELT!

Fly with us on the luxurious Carabuga space shuttle (leaves every Tuesday at 12.45) and you will spend six days travelling to the asteroid belt which is between Mars and Jupiter. You will also spend one night in the Olympus Hotel, Mars.

Once at the asteroid belt, the fun begins. For two days your instructor will teach you how to asteroid surf, and then you will be able to sail through space on your own board.

But – beware of flying rocks!!!

SURF THE BELT!

COSTS AND DATES

DATE	Basic Cost[1]	Insurance[2]	Extra night on Mars	Surfboard hire
1 Jan–31 March	Cr4250	Cr140	Cr100	Cr120 each
1 April–31 Aug	Cr3480	Cr140	Cr200 each	Cr120 each
1 Sept–31 Dec	Cr3190	Cr140	Cr100 each	Cr120 each

[1] All prices are given in Universal Credits.
[2] Insurance is compulsory.

From *Imaginative Projects* by Matt Wicks © Cambridge University Press 2000 **PHOTOCOPIABLE**

CUSTOMER CARDS

1A You want an adventurous holiday with your family, but you cannot really afford anything too expensive. (2500 Credits is your maximum.)

1B You want to go on an adventurous holiday with your family. You are not worried about how much it costs, but you know that your husband/wife is very worried about money.

2A You want something romantic and quiet, but you can only have three weeks off work.

2B You want to go somewhere with your girlfriend/boyfriend that is romantic and quiet. You have six weeks' holiday. You want her/him to stay with you for all six weeks.

3A You want something that will be good for your children. They have five weeks' summer holiday and you want to spend as much time as possible away from Earth.

3B You have five weeks' summer holiday and you want to stay on Earth with your friends, but your mother and father want to take you on holiday somewhere.

4A You hate travelling in shuttles because it makes you feel sick. In fact, you don't even like travelling on a bus because you think it goes too quickly.

4B You want to go on holiday with your friend. Your dream holiday is to take a long cruise around the solar system in a shuttle.

5A You are very rich and have done everything – you've been to Mars, Venus, Saturn, etc. You don't care how much it costs but you really want to do something exciting.

5B Every year your partner takes you on an 'exciting' holiday. This year you want to go somewhere quiet so that you can relax and read your books.

6A You want to go somewhere with your two friends, but they want different things. You want something connected with sport.

6B You want to go somewhere with your two friends, but they want different things. You want to see famous historical monuments.

6C You want to go somewhere with your two friends, but they want to do different things. You want to earn some money.

Topic area
the future, aliens, games

Language focus
questions
general revision

Key vocabulary
depends on revision
questions

Skills
speaking
pronunciation
(See page 15 for extra
activity on game play.)

Level
intermediate
(but easily adaptable to
any level)

Time
40 minutes

Materials
2 x dice
2 x page 53
photocopied and cut up
1 x page 54
photocopied and cut up
double the amounts
above for a large class

3.4 Loving the alien

Before class

1   Photocopy and cut up page 53 twice (or four times for a large class).

2   Photocopy and cut up page 54 once (or twice for a large class).

3   To make this game work really well, it is a good idea to write a few of your own cards to add to the piles so that students are revising structures or lexis which you have recently covered.

In class

1   Make sure that students are familiar with language connected with game play (see page 15).

2   Tell the students that a group of aliens has decided to attack Space City – mankind's first city in space. The only way to save millions of lives is for the brave defenders – i.e. half the students – to defeat the aliens (the other half). This is done by winning this game.

3   Divide the class into two groups – the humans and the aliens. (In really large classes you may need to set up two groups of each.)

4   Each group receives five appropriate rockets (i.e. aliens get alien rockets) from photocopiable page 53. The teacher keeps the remaining rockets to hand out later (see Step 6).

5   Both groups roll the dice once. The group with the highest numbers starts.

6   Write the following chart on the board:

```
DICE ROLLS:
1/3: Question card
2/4: Word card
5/6: Task card
```

7   The first group rolls the dice. The other group then selects a card from the appropriate pile (made up of the cards from page 54), as indicated in the chart.

8   The group that rolled the dice must then answer the question or perform the task on the card. If they answer correctly, or perform well, they receive another rocket (either from you or from a pile in the centre of the table). If they get the answer wrong or do not complete the task well, they lose a rocket.

9   The first group to get 20 rockets wins. Or, if one group loses all their rockets, the other group wins.

Variation
Younger students may enjoy designing their own aliens before doing this activity. They draw a picture of an imagined alien. They then describe the alien to their partner, who has to draw it, without looking at the original. Next they compare versions. This helps set the mood, especially if the pictures are pinned up around the room.

HUMAN CARDS

HUMAN HUMAN HUMAN HUMAN HUMAN

HUMAN HUMAN HUMAN HUMAN HUMAN

HUMAN HUMAN HUMAN HUMAN HUMAN

HUMAN HUMAN HUMAN HUMAN HUMAN

ALIEN CARDS

ALIEN ALIEN ALIEN ALIEN ALIEN

  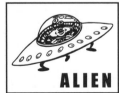 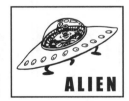 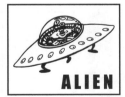
ALIEN ALIEN ALIEN ALIEN ALIEN

ALIEN ALIEN ALIEN ALIEN ALIEN

 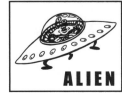   
ALIEN ALIEN ALIEN ALIEN ALIEN

TASK CARDS

Count from 187 to 218 without stopping.	Draw a mouse on the board.
The book costs £2.90. I give you £4.50. How much change should you give me?	Recite the alphabet.
Spell 'behaviour'.	Spell 'through'.
Name six countries in Europe and their nationalities. (e.g. Portugal / Portuguese)	Name the colours in the rainbow.
Sing three lines of a song that you know in English.	Tell us how to get to your house from the school.
Describe your bedroom.	If you were stuck on a desert island, which songs would you like to take with you?
Pretend to be a chimpanzee having a meal.	Draw a large hippopotamus on the board.

WORD CARDS

We advised the aliens. We warned the aliens. What is the difference?	Name three sports that you play and one that you do.
Who do you admire and why?	Think of four words to describe a friend of yours.
Name four things that you would take to the beach with you on a very hot day.	What do we call it when an aeroplane leaves the ground?
If I say that you are sensitive, what do I mean?	Think of four different words to describe the weather today.
Tell me a superstition.	A bottle of wine, a piece of paper, a ...... of bread, a ...... of chocolate, a ...... of fruit.
'Hello. Here is an ...... to my party. I hope you can come.'	Make a sentence using the verb 'make up'.
Make a sentence using the verb 'get off'.	Tell me something that you think is disgusting.

QUESTION CARDS

What aren't you allowed to do at home?	Which countries have you been to?
What do you look like? Describe yourself.	What is your best friend like?
What do you think will happen to Space City if the aliens win?	What are you going to do as soon as you get home tonight?
Do you know where your teacher lives?	What would you do if you were the President of your country?
Who was the Eiffel Tower in Paris built by?	Have you ever seen a horror movie?
What is the mistake in this question: Are you going to play football this night?	If you could travel in time, which year would you like to visit and why?
What is the missing word: "I'm eighteen – I'm old ...... to vote and get married!"	'I am going to eat you!' said the alien. What did the alien say?

4 The exhibition

LEVEL: Elementary–upper-intermediate

USING THIS PROJECT: In this project students make four separate exhibitions which can be compiled into one large exhibition. In each case there is an activity in which the students are both creators and spectators. However, if you do the whole project, the finale should be opening the entire spectacle to an outside audience and getting them to look at the exhibits: the pictures (4.1), the machines (4.2) and the fashion displays (4.3/4.4).

Those involved show other students around the exhibition, tell the stories behind the pictures or explain the machine. Alternatively, students produce a guide book which visitors read as they go round the exhibition.

	4.1 Three little pictures	**4.2** Make my machine	**4.3** Opening the wardrobe	**4.4** Catwalk
SKILLS	• speaking • writing	• writing • speaking	• speaking	• speaking
TIME	45–75 minutes	90–120 minutes	30–45 minutes	c. 105 minutes
PREPARATION	• getting pens and paper • optional: photocopying • enlarging • cutting up	• finding art materials • photocopying	• photocopying, • enlarging • cutting up • optional: finding different styles of music	• finding old clothes • finding fashion pictures in magazines
CLASS SIZE	2 plus	4–10 (more than 10 if you have a large space)	6 plus	6 plus (ideally 10 plus)
PAGE NUMBER	56	58	60	63

Topic area
stories, people, art

Language focus
narrative tenses
optional: contrast and
reporting verbs (see
Variation)

Key vocabulary
depends on the stories

Skills
speaking
writing

Level
pre-intermediate +

Time
45 minutes (speaking
only)
75 minutes (with
writing option)
(although it may be
more if you have a very
large class)

Materials
paper
pens to draw with
optional: I x picture
cards on page 57
enlarged and cut up

4.1 Three little pictures

Before class

1   Think of a funny story that has happened to you at some point in your life (or invent one, it doesn't really matter).

2   Draw this story as three pictures (like a cartoon strip) on the board / OHP.

3   Alternatively use the pictures and story from photocopiable page 57. Simply enlarge the pictures, cut them up and memorise the story.

In class

1   Ask the students to look at your pictures and see if they can guess what happened in your story. They can ask you as many questions as they want and you should answer, but try not to give away too much information at any one time.

2   If they are finding it difficult, give them a few clues – point to the parts of the picture which are most important and make certain that they know what the item is called. Ask them to imagine what might happen in this place / with this thing.

3   Once the students have guessed most of the tale, tell it to them and use the pictures to show them how the pictures are related to the story, if they haven't guessed.

4   Now give each student three pieces of paper and ask them to think of something that happened to them (or to make something up), and to draw a sequence of pictures to illustrate the event. Tell them that the quality of drawing really doesn't matter. Make sure that they do not show their pictures to any other students (you may need to send some of them into a different room).

5   When they have finished, collect all the pictures and hang them around the room in a random order.

6   Students walk around and rearrange the exhibition until it makes sense. In other words, tell them to find the groups of three which they think belong together and to put them all together in one place on the wall. They cannot touch or talk about their own pictures.

7   Once all of the groups of pictures are together, assign one student to each group of pictures (not their own). They have to look at the pictures and work out what the story behind them is.

8   The students tell the rest of the class their imagined stories for the pictures. The student who originally drew each picture then corrects as necessary.

Variation

For higher-level work on contrast in writing and reporting verbs: the student who looked at the picture (in Step 7) must write a text telling the story as he/she originally thought of it, but including the corrections that the student who drew the story made. For example, 'I thought that Jenny went to a market, but she told me that she went to a beach.'

Follow up

The student who looked at the pictures (Step 7) then has to write a short text about the correct story to put under the pictures (like the notices under paintings in galleries).

SAMPLE STORY

THE STORY

PICTURE 1: I used to live in Rome, a beautiful and very romantic city. One day in the middle of summer, I took my girlfriend to a huge tower because we wanted to watch the sunset. We climbed and climbed and climbed until we got to the top and then just stood there, looking at the sun going down. We stayed there for over an hour because it was so beautiful and peaceful.

PICTURE 2: After a while, my girlfriend started to feel cold and we decided to go back inside. Everywhere was dark and we became a little nervous. Carefully we went down the stairs … and more stairs … and more stairs. Until, finally, we got to the bottom … and discovered that the door was locked! We were trapped!

PICTURE 3: We didn't know what to do. We tried banging on the door, but it didn't work! We tried shouting, but it didn't work! We even tried turning the lights on and off to attract attention from outside. Finally, a VERY angry man came and opened the door. We smiled and pretended that we didn't speak any Italian at all. Unfortunately, my girlfriend was Italian and had gone to school with the angry man's son. He recognised her and chased us away.

4.2 Make my machine

Topic area
inventions, science

Language focus
instructions
zero conditional

Key vocabulary
press, push, pull, lift,
button, lever, belt, wheel

Skills
writing
speaking

Level
pre-intermediate–
intermediate

Time
90–120 mins

Materials
1 x machine worksheet
on page 59
photocopied per
student
old boxes, egg boxes,
etc.
bottles
paper
newspaper
toilet rolls
elastic bands
glue
scissors
optional: paint and any
other art materials that
are easy to get
(See page 13 for extra
activity.)

Before class

1 Gather together a selection of materials that students can use to make things in the class. This includes old boxes, toilet rolls, old pieces of card. It is a good idea to get the students to bring in some bits and pieces as well.

2 Check that you have enough tubes of glue, pairs of scissors, rolls of sellotape, etc. for your class.

3 Photocopy one machine worksheet on page 59 for each student. Cut the answers to the text off before handing out the worksheets.

In class

1 Make sure that students are familiar with classroom language connected with making and doing (see page 13). In addition, they need to know what *push, pull, press* and *lift* mean (these can easily be demonstrated or mimed by you or members of the class while others identify them).

2 Put the students into pairs and give each student a copy of page 59. They should work through it, filling in the missing words.

3 Once they have completed the text and labelled the diagram, each pair has to guess what the machine does.

4 After everybody has guessed, tell them the answer: it is designed to teach people in three minutes all the English they need to pass their exams!

5 Now tell the students that they are going to design their own machines. They can invent machines to do anything.

6 Elicit some ideas for things that they hate doing and for which they would like to have a machine (things such as tying your shoelaces, tidying your room, etc.). Warn them that somebody is going to have to make their machine out of toilet rolls and cardboard so that they shouldn't be too ambitious.

7 Using the text on photocopiable page 59 as a model, each pair should write a short text of their own describing what their machine does, and how it does it. ('First, push button number one. A green light comes on', etc.) They should not draw anything at this point.

8 When they have finished, collect in all the papers.

9 Hand the papers out again to other students along with the materials to make the machines – old packets, sticks, plastic bottles, magazines, etc. They will also need glue or sellotape and perhaps some paint.

10 Their task is to make the machine described on their piece of paper. It does not have to be perfect, but they should make certain that all the buttons, levers, etc., are in place more or less as described.

11 When each group has completed the task, you can set up an exhibition corner of strange inventions. The designers of each machine can then look at the finished product and see if they think it will perform the function that it is supposed to.

Variation

This activity works well with younger students. If you have older students, then get them to draw their ideas for machines. Instead of making the machines (Steps 9–10) they can create 'blueprints' of them in technical detail using rulers, protractors and compasses. This can also be a useful way of practising numbers and measurements.

MACHINE WORKSHEET

Fill in the information about my machine below, using these words:

button   lever   pull   push   lifts   belt   wheel   turns

How my machine works

First, you press _____ one to start it. Then you _____ lever one and the big wheel turns. When the big wheel _____ , the _____ also moves and this makes the little wheel turn. The little _____ sends energy to the helmet. To increase the power, press button two, and _____ lever three. When you pull lever three, the helmet _____ off. You put your head in the helmet and press button three. Finally, you pull _____ two and the machine begins to work.

Now label the diagram to show the buttons, levers, helmet, etc.

- -

Answers to text

First, you press *button* one to start it. Then you *push* lever one and the big wheel turns. When the big wheel *turns*, the *belt* also moves and this makes the little wheel turn. The little *wheel* sends energy to the helmet. To increase the power, press button two, and *pull* lever three. When you pull lever three, the helmet *lifts* off. You put your head in the helmet and press button three. Finally, you pull *lever* two and the machine begins to work.

Topic area
fashion, clothes, people

Language focus
descriptions

Skills
speaking

Level
elementary–pre-intermediate (using page 61)
intermediate–upper-intermediate (using page 62)

Time
30 mins
45 mins for higher levels if doing follow-up activity

Materials
1 x page 61 enlarged and cut up (lower levels)
1 x page 62 enlarged and cut up (higher levels)
optional: different styles of music (higher levels)

Note This exercise is designed to be done with 4.4 and, although it can be done alone, it works better when followed up by 4.4.

4.3 Opening the wardrobe

Before class
1 If you have a lower-level group, you will need to photocopy, enlarge and cut up page 61. For a higher-level class, photocopy, enlarge and cut up page 62.

2 If you are going to do the follow-up activity, you will also need to bring in different types of music to illustrate the cults that are on the cards.

In class
1 Stick the enlarged cards from page 61 or page 62 around the room.

2 Put the students into pairs and tell each pair that one picture 'belongs' to them. Ideally, their picture should be positioned a short distance away from them. Make sure that each student is quite clear which picture is theirs.

3 Explain that you are going to say a word. If a picture of that word (for example, *skirt)* is in their picture, they run to the picture and write the word on the paper with an arrow pointing to the correct place. Draw an example on the board.

4 When they are ready, you can start calling out the words from the appropriate list. Call them out in any order you choose. Once groups have written their word, they sit in silence. Read the next word when all the groups are silent and ready.

5 The first group to label all the clothes on their picture correctly wins. When they think they have finished, they call out *'Finished'* and bring the picture to you. However, you should continue reading until all the groups have finished.

6 Now pass all the pictures around so that other groups can see them. If an item has been incorrectly labelled, help the group who labelled it to correct the error.

7 When everybody has seen all of the pictures, elicit what types of design it is possible to have on clothes (e.g. stripes, checks, spots, etc.). Write these on the board and illustrate them where possible by pointing to clothing round the class.

8 One person in the group starts this part of the exercise by describing two things from an imaginary outfit they are 'wearing'. In a weaker class, it will need to be modelled by the teacher, e.g. *I am wearing a striped dress and blue spotted shoes* even if in fact you are wearing a blue skirt and black shoes. Each example sentence should include at least one colour and one pattern.

9 The next person repeats what the previous one said, e.g. *Leslie is wearing a striped dress and blue spotted shoes*, and continues … *and I am wearing some checked trousers and a pink striped shirt*. Students must not write anything down during this game. The game continues until somebody forgets something, when you can begin again. If students think that someone has made an error, they may suggest corrections. In a large class, you will need two groups.

Follow up
The cards for the higher-level students are all based on various fashion 'cults'. If you can, bring in some music and see if they can match the type of music with the picture (e.g. 'The Beatles' goes with 'Hippie', etc.). Also, write a list of the names of the various 'cults' on the board and see if they can match them with the pictures/music. (They are, in order of appearance on page 62: Hippie, Skinhead, Breakdancer, Punk, Goth and Raver.) You can adapt this list to suit the available music or particular cults in your country. This activity can be followed up by a comparison with their own teenage experiences – are there any similar movements based on music? What do they wear, etc.? What type of fashions are popular in your local area? This can lead to some interesting multi-cultural discussion work in mixed nationality classes.

LOWER-LEVEL FASHION CARDS

Lower-level groups

Read these words to your students in any order:

jeans   jacket   earrings   hat   belt
high-heeled shoes   waistcoat   tie   flat shoes   trainers
umbrella   collar   glasses   trousers   skirt
shorts   suit   coat   T-shirt   necklace

HIGHER-LEVEL FASHION CARDS

 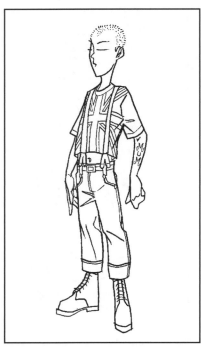 

From *Imaginative Projects* by Matt Wicks © Cambridge University Press 2000 **PHOTOCOPIABLE**

Higher-level groups

Read these words to your students in any order:

leggings   T-shirt   trousers   earrings   gloves
headband   tracksuit   bracelets   boots   jeans
braces   leather jacket   belt   tattoo   mini skirt
tights   hood   sandals   trainers

4.4 Catwalk

Topic area
fashion, people, media

Language focus
descriptions
present continuous
colours

Key vocabulary
see 4.3; also specific
words relating to the
clothes students bring in

Skills
speaking

Level
elementary–
upper-intermediate

Time
Lesson 1: 45 minutes
(but see note below)
Lesson 2: 60 minutes

Materials
fashion pictures from
magazines
old clothes
optional: video camera
and cassette or photo
camera
optional: music for the
fashion display

Note This exercise is
designed for use with
4.3. Although it can be
done separately, a lot of
the language can be pre-
taught by using 4.3.

Before class

1 Gather together pictures and magazines of recent fashions.

2 For lesson 2, it is a good idea to bring in some clothes yourself. Anybody who doesn't bring their own clothes will still be able to participate. As always, if you enter into the spirit of it, students are much more likely to follow.

In class

1 Do 4.3: Opening the wardrobe to pre-teach vocabulary.

2 *Lesson 1*
Ask students to describe what is fashionable this year. Make a list, using pictures from magazines to help generate ideas. Try to elicit types of clothes, patterns, materials and colours.
You could send the students out to local shops to look in the windows and see what is most popular. If they are in an English-speaking country, encourage them to speak to shop owners. (This could be done as homework.)

3 Put the students into groups of five or six. Tell them that they are going to create their own fashion show.

4 Get them to think about what is going to be fashionable in the future. Encourage them to be inventive. What colours will be popular? Will big hats be worn? What about ties for men? Skirt lengths?

5 Once they have thought about these things, one person is chosen as the commentator and the rest as the models. They draw up a list of the clothes that each student must bring in for the next lesson's fashion show.

6 The students must leave this lesson with a clear idea of the clothes that they need to bring in for the next lesson. They should bring either clothes that are kept for special occasions, or embarrassing things that they now hate to wear. The purpose is to have fun and exaggerate rather than to be too serious, otherwise more self-conscious members of the class may not want to join in.

7 *Lesson 2*
Make a 'catwalk' by pushing tables back, or move your desk and use the front of the classroom.

8 The students each present their fashion show with the models walking around the catwalk.

9 At the same time, the commentator describes what each person is wearing (including the colour and maybe the material for a higher level).

10 If possible, the show should be recorded or videoed. Students look at the recording for errors of pronunciation or vocabulary. You can also suggest ways in which the description could be extended. *Luigia is wearing a yellow dress*, could become *Luigia is wearing a fantastic yellow dress, suitable for the summer*.

Variation

Some older groups, especially with a lot of boys, might feel this activity is too young for them. In this case, get the students to imagine that they are joining some sort of organisation that requires a uniform. The fact that they are all trying to work together to agree on one design rather than on any different 'fashionable' designs will generally bring people into the activity. The uniform can be a simple school one, a military one or a futuristic one. It depends very much on the interests of the students.

Some students on the catwalk in Portugal

5 Blind date

LEVEL: Pre-intermediate–advanced

USING THIS PROJECT: This project tells the story of a relationship. It begins with getting a date (5.1), follows through with the actual date (5.2), then comes the love story (5.3), and finally the honeymoon (5.4).

Thematically, teenagers generally get quite involved in this project. However, in certain cultures these ideas may be inappropriate. For this reason, each section of this project contains alternative ideas for using the materials.

As with 'Movie moguls', some aspects of this project (notably the photo story, 5.3) require an autonomous group capable of working independently and with minimal supervision.

Time limits are also important – time for answering questions should be limited in 5.1, and the amount of time students have to take photos in 5.3 should be carefully organised and controlled as well. It is important to remember that, fun as these activities are, there is a linguistic element to each one which must be kept in focus.

	5.1 **Getting a date**	**5.2** **The date**	**5.3** **Photo love**	**5.4** **Honeymoon**
SKILLS	● speaking	● speaking ● writing	● speaking ● writing	● speaking ● reading
TIME	30 or 60 minutes	20 minutes per pair who 'perform'	2½–3½ hours over 3 lessons	35–45 minutes
PREPARATION	● photocopying ● cutting up	● organising classroom	● photocopying ● getting cameras and films	● photocopying ● cutting up
CLASS SIZE	8 plus	6 plus	4 plus (ideally with 6–14)	4 plus
PAGE NUMBER	66	68	69	72

5.1 Getting a date

Before class

1 If you are doing the shorter version of this activity (see Step 4) then photocopy and cut up the cards on page 67.

2 Think about (and possibly arrange) how the classroom will be set up for the actual 'competition' part of the lesson.

In class

1 Explain to your students that they are going to find 'dates' for themselves. This is done by one female selecting from a choice of three males whose identities are kept secret. The female asks three questions and the males answer them. From those answers she selects her date. The process is then repeated with a male choosing from three females.

2 Write *'If we were on holiday together and I wanted to visit a place that you hated, what would you do?'* on the board. Elicit some sample answers from the students. Write some of their answers on the board. Pay attention to accuracy at this point, focusing on the use of *would* to indicate a hypothetical situation.

3 Hand out blank cards for your students and ask them to write two or three questions that they would like to ask a potential partner. They follow the model you have provided. Then, collect them in and mix them up. Or for speed, use the prepared cards on page 67.

4 Now the male and female students have to be separated into different rooms (or at least send one group into the corridor for a little while).

5 The males choose three 'contestants' and the females choose one 'contestant'. All the contestants give themselves fake names because their identities must be kept secret. These names will be used by the compère (either the teacher or a confident student) during the 'show'.

6 The female students are then given five question cards which their elected contestant reads out. The three elected males must answer the questions as fully as they can.
If students don't know each other well: Erect a barrier between the two groups to conceal identities. Students can also disguise their voices.
If students know each other well: Keep groups in separate rooms with the non-contesting students acting as 'messengers', running between them repeating questions and answers so as to preserve the secret identities. You may need to intervene occasionally but that can be done in the character of a compère.

7 Once the questions and answers have all been completed the female students gather around and help the contestant select the male they think would be the most suitable date for her.

8 The process is then repeated with three female students answering questions and one male asking them.

Variation

If this exercise is culturally inappropriate for your group, divide the class into two halves. One group asks the questions and the other answers. Instead of using the questions on page 67, the students can write their own *would* questions using any situations they choose. *'What would you do if you were asked to play football for your country?'* etc. In this case, the losing team is the first team that cannot think of an answer to their opponents' questions.

Topic area
relationships, media, drama, people

Language focus
second conditional hypothetical language questions

Key vocabulary
date, seeing someone, bully

Skills
speaking

Level
intermediate–advanced

Time
short version: 30 mins
long version: 60 mins

Materials
1 x cut up cards on page 67 for short version
pens
blank cards for long version
optional: some sort of classroom divider

BLIND DATE QUESTIONS

I like going to the cinema. If I wanted to go to the cinema and see a film that you hated, what would you do?

I love computer games. If you were a computer game, what type of computer game would you be?

If it was our first date together, would you rather go somewhere romantic or somewhere fun? Why?

Imagine that we were having dinner in a very expensive restaurant. Suddenly I felt very sick. What would you do?

What would you do if we were having dinner in a very expensive restaurant and I realised that I had forgotten my wallet / purse and all my money / credit cards?

What would you do if I bought you a very expensive pair of trousers for your birthday, but you hated them?

I love animals. If you were an animal, what sort of animal would you be and why?

If you discovered that my brother was bullying other students at school, would you tell me about it or not? Why?

What would you do if we had been seeing each other for six months and then a beautiful/handsome movie star suddenly invited you to a party?

I like expensive clothes. What would you do if we were walking past a shop one day and I saw a fantastic pair of designer jeans for £450 and asked you to buy them for me?

5.2 The date

Topic areas
food, relationships, people, drama

Language focus
question forms functional restaurant language (See also 7.3.)

Key vocabulary
date, to go out together as required by the script writers

Skills
speaking
writing

Level
pre-intermediate–advanced

Time
20 minutes per pair who 'perform'

Materials
pens
strips of paper
food
optional: menu made up from template on page 89

Before class

1 Cut up several pieces of paper into strips (about a quarter of a page in size).

2 Bring in some food and cups for drinks.

3 If you wish to create the atmosphere of a candle-lit restaurant, then you will need to bring in tablecloths and can also make menus up from the template on page 89. It will take some time, but is well worth the result.

In class

1 Get the students to set the classroom up as a restaurant. The more detail the better, so having real food, darkened lights, and a tablecloth would be perfect. The table should have two seats. Behind each seat the rest of the chairs should be equally divided (making two teams on opposite sides of the room).

2 Either use the two winners of the 'Getting a date' exercise (5.1) or choose two volunteers and explain that they are on a date.

3 If you have a large class, set up two or three different pairs of daters.

4 Now divide the rest of the class so that half of them are sitting behind person A and half behind person B. In a large class, divide the class so that there are equal numbers of people behind each dater.

5 Tell A and B that they can only do what they are told to do, or say what they are told to say, by the people sitting behind them.

6 You will need to give an example. Write on the board. *A: Hi, nice to see you.* A must then say *'Hi, nice to see you.'* Then write *B: Hello. (eats)* B then says *'Hello'* and eats something.

7 The students (in the groups behind the daters) then take over, writing lines of dialogue and passing them to the daters in sequence, not forgetting directions such as eating, smiling, laughing, coughing, etc. or important things in a restaurant such as ordering food.

8 This continues as long as it is sustainable. You can add suggestions, and direct them towards romantic phrases and questions for the waiter. If the script requires a third person to become the waiter for a short while, then get a volunteer to do it. However, make sure the focus stays mainly on the two people at the table.

9 Once the activity starts to slow down (usually after about 10–15 minutes), direct the students to conclude the date somehow.

10 To finish the exercise, the two daters should read through the completed script once again from start to finish to give a sense of the whole piece.

11 The students can then take the script that they have written, put it together, edit it and rewrite it. This will give them a script that they can use for pronunciation and speaking work, as well as a completed written piece of work which has had input from everybody.

12 The exercise should then be repeated with another couple or the other winners of the 'Getting a date' section.

Variation

In certain cultures or with younger age groups, this activity may not be appropriate. In this case, you can replace the two daters by two friends. Set up a situation (e.g. they are arguing, they are planning to rob a bank, they are worried about their exams) and follow through Steps 4–9 above.

5.3 Photo love

Topic areas

relationships, media, people, art

Language focus

instructions
Vocabulary will vary from group to group.

Key vocabulary

photo story, to play a character, to dress up as cameras: *lens, to take a picture, focus* pronunciation and stress of 'photograph vs. pho'tographer, etc.

Skills

speaking
writing

Level

intermediate–advanced

Time

Lesson 1: 45 minutes
Lesson 2: 60–120 minutes
Allow time to get the photos developed.
Lesson 3: 45 minutes

Materials

pens
1 x page 70 and page 71 per 6 students
paper
1 x camera and film per group
card (for mounting display) and glue

Before class

This activity is based on the photo love stories traditionally found in teenage magazines, and generally works better if done as humorously as possible.
You could buy a teenage magazine with a photo story in it to show the students.

In class

1 *Lesson 1* Establish what photo stories are. Show an example if you can, from a teenage magazine.

2 Divide the class into groups of six or seven (fewer if your class is small). Tell them that they are going to plan and make their own photo story. Give each group a copy of the planning sheet (pages 70–71).

3 Point to the first heading (1. First meeting) and write it on the board. Elicit situations two people of the opposite sex might meet in and make a list.

4 As a group, choose one of these situations and get everyone to think of what might happen at this meeting. This should be described in three to four sentences and written in the first two boxes on the planning sheet.

5 Elicit ideas of where they could photograph the two pictures and add the location to the 'Where are we going to take the photo?' section of the first two boxes.

6 Now send students off in their groups to make up a story following the five headings on the planning sheet. (They can use the 'First meeting' that everybody has thought of together or they can invent a new one.)

7 Once they have the framework of the story, the groups discuss details: who is going to play which character? What are they going to wear? Each group should make a cast and costume list to add to the planning sheet.

8 Tell students to bring in appropriate clothes for the next lesson. Bring in some of your own, too. There is always someone who forgets.

9 *Lesson 2* Send the students out in costume to take the photographs. Encourage them to stick to their plan in general, but allow for improvisation in details. (See the note about timing.)

10 Get the film developed.

11 *Lesson 3* Get the students to mount the developed pictures on card in order and then to add the dialogue. They can use the speech balloons on page 71 for this. Suggest they work out what they want to say in rough, first.

12 Finally, add in any explanatory phrases / notes under the photographs that they (or you) think necessary. Don't forget to give it a suitable (funny) title.

Variation

In cultures where such a relationship is inappropriate, change the story. It could be a bank raid with the pictures showing: 1. The plan 2. Approaching the bank 3. The robbery 4. The pursuit and 5. Capture.

Photo love plan

1. First meeting

Picture 1
What happens?

. . . .
. . . .
. . . .

Where are we going to take the photos?

. . . .
. . . .

Picture 2
What happens?

. . . .
. . . .
. . . .

Where are we going to take the photos?

. . . .
. . . .

2. Argument!

Picture 3
What happens?

. . . .
. . . .
. . . .

Where are we going to take the photos?

. . . .
. . . .

Picture 4
What happens?

. . . .
. . . .
. . . .

Where are we going to take the photos?

. . . .
. . . .

3. All alone!

Picture 5
What happens?

. . . .
. . . .
. . . .

Where are we going to take the photos?

. . . .
. . . .

Picture 6
What happens?

. . . .
. . . .
. . . .

Where are we going to take the photos?

. . . .
. . . .

From *Imaginative Projects* by Matt Wicks © Cambridge University Press 2000 **PHOTOCOPIABLE**

4. Saying sorry

Picture 7
What happens?

. . . .
. . . .
. . . .

Where are we going to take the photos?

. . . .
. . . .

Picture 8
What happens?

. . . .
. . . .
. . . .

Where are we going to take the photos?

. . . .
. . . .

5. The end

Picture 9
What happens?

. . . .
. . . .
. . . .

Where are we going to take the photos?

. . . .
. . . .

Picture 10
What happens?

. . . .
. . . .
. . . .

Where are we going to take the photos?

. . . .
. . . .

5.4 Honeymoon

Topic area
travel, relationships

Language focus
likes and dislikes
making suggestions
agreeing and
disagreeing

Key vocabulary
honeymoon, scorpion,
snowball, sledge, mall,
to camp, hammock,
dolphin, give up, surf,
instructor, camel

Skills
speaking (See page 17
for extra activity.)
reading

Level
intermediate +

Time
35–45 minutes

Materials
1 x cut up set of cards
on page 73 and page 74
per pair

Before class
Photocopy and cut up one set of cards on pages 73 and 74 for each pair.

In class

1   Check that the students are familiar with the classroom language connected with speaking activities (see page 17).

2   Elicit the word *honeymoon* and some suggestions of where people might go on their honeymoons.

3   Explain to the students that they are going to choose their honeymoon destination. Put them in pairs. As far as possible try to mix the genders up. If it is impossible to have a reasonable boy–girl match, or such an exercise is culturally inappropriate, then use the *Variation* below.

4   Give each group ten of the 16 cards on photocopiable pages 73 and 74. (It doesn't matter which ten, but try to make sure that all cards are used at least once.)

5   The pairs have to read the cards and decide which honeymoon they would like to go on together. They will need to think about how long each trip is for, where it is, what the climate is like and whether or not they both have something to do.

6   Once they have reached an agreement everybody can report back. You should go through each card individually, getting one pair to explain to the rest what type of holiday it was, whether or not they chose it and why (or why not). As they speak, list the destinations on the board.

7   When the students have spoken about all 16 possibilities, give them a couple of minutes in their original pairs to see if they would like to change their choice (because they now have 16 rather than ten holidays to choose from).

Variation
If romance is not appropriate for your class for cultural or age reasons, then the activity can still be done with the students choosing the holiday that they prefer rather than the honeymoon. In this case, there is no need to restrict the group to pairs – they can work in threes or fours, which promotes even more discussion.

Follow up
Students can make up their own cards with their own ideal honeymoon on it. (Keep a copy to use with subsequent groups.)

HONEYMOON CARDS

A week for two in MEXICO! Ride horses. Learn how cowboys really live. Camp out every night. Meet scorpions and snakes. The adventure of a lifetime.

Travel the whole of Asia in a balloon. Your feet won't touch the ground for seven days! You will see birds and aeroplanes very close up!

Two weeks in Iceland. The temperature is minus 25 degrees ... WOW! You can have snowball fights, use a sledge, make snowmen and women – even in the middle of summer!

Take your friends and go shopping! Yes, that is right: one week, just SHOPPING! All you have to do is arrive (with lots of money). We'll drive you in a bus from shopping mall to shopping mall. Most days, we stop at three malls! What a fantastic opportunity.

Ten days in New Zealand, camping, cooking outside and swimming with a DOLPHIN every day.

Three weeks on an island with nothing to do except sunbathe all day and drink cold drinks as you relax in your hammock.

Climb Mont Blanc. Only you and your partner, with no guide – just one map, some skis and a rope. Can you reach the top in a week? Or will you give up halfway up?

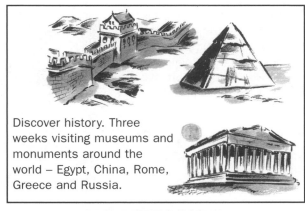

Discover history. Three weeks visiting museums and monuments around the world – Egypt, China, Rome, Greece and Russia.

HONEYMOON CARDS

 CLUB FRED 14–24. Enjoy a week on the beach in Greece with people of your own age. Lots of football. Lots of beautiful people. Parties every night.

 Three weeks on a camel travelling in North Africa. You, your camel, the guide and sand, sand, sand. What a perfect holiday.

Two weeks at the Cannes Film Festival: see all the movies and have dinner with the stars.

 VENICE. A romantic weekend for two on the canals of Venice.

 WATERSPORTS. Spend a week at our special lake and you can try a lot of new water sports: swimming, sailing, surfing, water skiing, or diving. Anything you want to do – with water.

 Spend ten days in Japan learning about sushi, sake, sumo and the traditional Japanese way of life.

SKI SEASON. Spend a fortnight in Switzerland, skiing or snowboarding in some of the most beautiful mountains in the world. Instruction, skis and weather all provided.

 Why not come on a safari in Kenya? Three weeks, lots of sun and you can meet me and my friends.

From *Imaginative Projects* by Matt Wicks © Cambridge University Press 2000 **PHOTOCOPIABLE**

6 Radio show

LEVEL: Intermediate–upper-intermediate

USING THIS PROJECT: The best way to do this project is to work on the separate activities as described and then tape them all onto a master tape for students to listen to at the end as one single radio broadcast.

Ideally, each student should be able to get their own copy to take home with them to show the success of the project. In addition, try to to find a good tape recorder with a plug-in microphone so that the sound quality is high. It will also make students feel more like radio presenters.

The structure of the finished product can vary, but one suggested order would be starting off with the news (6.4), followed by interviews (6.1) which can be set up / introduced by a DJ (a confident student or the teacher). The Harchards (6.3) can be recorded onto the master tape in episodes, fitted in between the interviews. Clearly, different students' versions of the Harchards will have to be used. It is unlikely, however, that you will want to include every single episode, so it is better to select the very best, or if you have a lot of time, to personalise each student's tape by recording their version of the Harchards onto it. Throughout the whole broadcast there will, of course, be advertising breaks (6.2).

In addition, the activity 'Desert island students' (1.3, page 24) could easily be incorporated here as a fun extra. Remember that not all the students have to be doing the same activity simultaneously – some can be doing 'Idols' while others are doing 'Adverts', and so on.

	6.1 Idols	6.2 Adverts	6.3 The Harchards	6.4 Headlines
SKILLS	● speaking ● writing	● speaking ● pronunciation	● speaking ● writing	● speaking ● writing
TIME	90 minutes	60 minutes	c. 100 minutes over 2 lessons	60 minutes
PREPARATION	● finding pictures of famous people ● photocopying	● finding adverts and trademarks ● photocopying	● photocopying	● making a recording ● photocopying
CLASS SIZE	2 plus	4 plus	5 plus	2 plus
PAGE NUMBER	76	78	80	82

6.1 Idols

Topic area
media, famous people, fashion

Language focus
question forms
past tenses
present perfect

Key vocabulary
idol, hero

Skills
speaking
writing

Level
intermediate +

Time
90 minutes or 90 minutes + homework (See Step 5.)

Materials
pictures of famous people
I x page 77 per student
tape recorder
tape
optional: microphone

Before class

1   Photocopy one page 77 for each student.

2   Collect pictures of famous people from various jobs (great leaders, pop stars, film stars, scientists, etc.) and pin them around the classroom.

In class

1   Ask the students to walk around the class looking at the pictures, but do not say anything about them. Try to elicit the names of as many as possible and what they are famous for.

2   Ask the students if they can guess what all these people have in common. If they cannot guess, explain that these people are 'idols' – heroes whom people look up to.

3   Put the students into groups of three or four and get them to tell each other who their idols are, and why. (Help them with ideas if necessary – football players, film stars, singers, etc.)

4   **The questions** Tell the class that they are going to interview their idols. In order to prepare for this, they will need to write the questions that they would like to ask. This part of the activity should be done individually.

5   **The answers** Now put the students into pairs for the interview. In the interview, Student B will play the role of Student A's idol, and vice versa. In order to do this, they need to do some preparation. There are two ways of doing this:

Short version: Students B fill in photocopiable page 77 with a mixture of information that Students A tell them about their idol.

Long version: Students B fill in photocopiable page 77 using research. This can include magazines, encyclopaedias and the Internet. This is best given as homework.

In either case, page 77 will provide the basis for the answers that the idol gives.

6   Students rehearse their interview. Students A read the questions and Students B answer from the information compiled in Step 5.

7   The interview is taped and students then change roles, rehearse and tape again.

8   Each student gives the rest of the class three of the questions that he/she asked his/her idol, either dictating them or writing them on the board.

9   As each interview is played back to the whole class, the rest of the students have to listen for the answers to the three questions. You or the student ask the class how much they heard or understood after playing the radio show.

IDOL INFORMATION PAGE

MY IDOL

PUT A PICTURE OF
YOUR IDOL HERE

Name: _____ Date of birth: _____

Place of birth: _____

Is this person still alive?_____

When did they die? _____

What is this person famous for (e.g. films, music, science, sport)?

_____ _____

Details:

_____

_____

_____

_____

_____

I admire this person because: _____

6.2 Adverts

Topic area
advertising, media, drama

Language focus
present simple
can (ability)
should

Key vocabulary
jingle

Skills
speaking
pronunciation

Level
intermediate–
upper-intermediate

Time
60 minutes

Materials
pictures or recordings
of adverts
1 x page 79 cut up
tape recorder
tape
optional: microphone

Before class

1   Collect a series of popular advertisements (pictures or videos) that you think your students will recognise.

2   Photocopy and cut up page 79.

3   If you feel confident, record the example advert on page 79 onto a tape, using dynamic intonation to attract your customers' attention.

In class

1   Show the students the adverts with the trademark/name hidden. They have to guess what the advert was for and comment on whether or not they liked it.

2   As a whole group, choose the adverts (from Step 1) which the class liked and ask them why. What makes a good advert: action? Colour? Speed? Beautiful people? etc. Write a list of good and bad points on the board.

3   Ask the students to think about how they can communicate all of this without pictures, i.e. how to make an effective radio advert. Draw their attention to things such as changing intonation, sound effects and repetition of the brand name.

4   Put the students into groups of four and tell each group that they are going to make a radio advert. The advert must last no longer than 30 seconds. They can include sound effects (as long as they can make them), jingles (you will need to explain what these are) and exciting intonation. Give them an example of the sort of thing you want them to do (there is one at the top of photocopiable page 79).

5   Once the students have the idea, give them a card from photocopiable page 79, or get them to think of their own products.

6   There are three steps to their 'advert': (a) working out the script (b) 'finding' the sound effects, and (c) creating a jingle. In total this will take about 40 minutes. They should complete each point and check with you before moving on to the next step.

7   Go around each group as they are working, using the opportunity to work on intonation and on individual sound pronunciation (which often arises out of the jingles).

8   Finally, the adverts are recorded and then played back to the whole group. At this point, you can correct general errors.

BRIAN'S BEANS

A whole meal in one bean!

NARRATOR: *Do you like beans?*
OTHERS: *Yes, we love beans.*
NARRATOR: *What sort of beans do you like?*
OTHERS: *We love Brian's beans.*
NARRATOR: *Why?*
OTHERS: *Well, when you open them (sound effect), they smell so good (sound effect), then you cook them (sound effect), and they taste GREAAAAT. (sound effect). And, . . .*
NARRATOR: *Yes?*
OTHERS: *They're very very cheap.*
JINGLE: *Buy Brian's Brilliant Beans The most brilliant beans you can buy.*

SAMMY'S FITNESS SWEETS
Have one sweet a day and you will always be healthy.

CAROL'S CRAZY CAR
It talks to you while you drive.

HARRY'S HOMEWORK MACHINE
It does your homework for you.

TERRY'S TIME SHIP
Travel back into history.

PETER'S POPPING POP
Drink this drink and you will become a pop star.

THOMAS' TINY TANK
A real tank that fits in your pocket.

SALLY'S SLIPPERY SLUG
Give this as a present to your ENEMY.

ROBERT'S RUBBER LORRY
This lorry is very safe! If you drive into anything it bounces back like a ball.

6.3 The Harchards

Topic areas
relationships, people, media, drama

Language focus
direct speech

Key vocabulary
soap opera, tap

Skills
speaking
writing

Level
intermediate (but can be adapted for pre-intermediate, see Variation)

Time
Lesson 1: 60 minutes
Lesson 2: 45 minutes

Materials
1 x page 81 per student
tape recorder
tape

Before class
Photocopy page 81 once for each student.

In class
1 *Lesson 1*
Hand out the copies of page 81, and get the students to read it through to themselves. Check students understand what a 'soap opera' is.

2 Drill the names of the characters to make certain that everybody can pronounce them.

The characters:	Pronunciation
Bob	/bɒb/
Susan	/ˈsuːzən/
Jemima	/dʒəˈmaimə/
George	/dʒɔːdʒ/
Julia	/ˈdʒuːliə/

3 Ask for volunteers to read the script aloud to the class. Read it aloud, pointing out the contractions as you go through.

4 Check that the students all understand who the characters are and what is happening. You could draw a chart on the board showing all of the relationships in pictorial form.

5 Divide the class into groups of four or five and tell them that they are going to record the next episode of the soap opera. In order to do that, they have to write another page of script, continuing the story.

6 Each group writes their text. Monitor, providing suggestions and correction where needed.

7 The groups cast the characters and practise reading their text.

8 Each group records themselves. These tapes can then be used for error correction.

9 *Lesson 2*
Ask the groups to write the final episode of the soap opera. This time, they have to continue from a different group's script. Thus, group A's script goes to group B, group B's to group C and so on. They have to write a page of script which satisfactorily concludes the story.

10 At the end of the activity, each group has three pages of script: photocopiable page 81, another group's second page and their own third page. They should then record the whole thing, taking into account the error correction given in Step 8.

11 Students can listen to the alternative versions and see how their own second pages were completed by their colleagues.

Variation
For a pre-intermediate group, it is enough to record page 81 two or three different times, focusing on changing stress and intonation as well as a more general comprehension of what is happening.

THE HARCHARDS: a soap opera

Episode 1

SCENE ONE
[SOUND EFFECT: Rain <Make this by recording water (from a tap) falling on something metal>]

BOB: Hello, Susan. How are you?
SUSAN: Oh Bob! Bob my darling! I'm so happy to see you.
BOB: Why? What happened?
SUSAN: Oh Bob! Bob, my sweetheart! It was terrible.
BOB: What happened?
SUSAN: George has found out our secret.
BOB: No!
SUSAN: Yes! Oh, Bob, my one true love! George – my terrible husband –
            has found out that I love you and not him.
BOB: That is awful.
SUSAN: Yes. And now, Bob, my handsome hero, he is coming here to kill you!
BOB: To kill me? Oh no! What can I do? What can I do?

SCENE TWO
[SOUND EFFECT: A door slamming, loudly]
JEMIMA: Mr George! Mr George! What's the matter?
GEORGE: Grrrrrrrrrr.
JEMIMA: Here, Mr George, have some coffee.
[SOUND EFFECT: Coffee being poured into a cup]
JEMIMA: And put the gun down. I've been your secretary for ten years
            and I've never seen you so angry!
GEORGE: My wife loves another man. She loves Bob the cleaner.
JEMIMA: I can't believe it.
GEORGE: It's true and when I've finished my coffee I'm going to shoot
            him. Bang! Bang! Bang! Bang! Bang! Bang!
JEMIMA: Oh, poor Mr George.
GEORGE: Don't cry, Jemima.
JEMIMA: But I have to Mr George. You see there's a secret I must tell
            you . . .

SCENE THREE
[SOUND EFFECT: A car arriving < Make this by saying 'Brrrrrmmmm' into the microphone>]
JULIA: Susan! Susan! Are you there?
SUSAN: Yes, Julia, here I am.
JULIA: How is Bob?
SUSAN: He is afraid. And George is angry
JULIA: Good, our plan is working. Your husband, George, is angry
            because Bob – my husband – loves you. George'll kill Bob, and
            then the police'll put George in prison. I'll get Bob's money
            and you'll get George's money.
SUSAN: HA HA HA HA HA HA HA HA HA!

To be continued

6.4 Headlines

Topic area
media, news, famous people

Language focus
past simple
present perfect
reported speech

Key vocabulary
headlines, correspondent, journalist, reporter, anchor

Skills
speaking
writing

Level
intermediate +

Time
60 minutes

Materials
1 x cut up headlines on page 83
tape recorder
tape
optional: microphone

Before class

1   Photocopy and cut up page 83.

2   Record the headlines from an English language news programmes. (If you are not in an English-speaking country, use the BBC World Service, which has news on the hour.)

In class

1   Ask the students to listen to the headlines and write them down. They will need to hear the headlines several times before getting them accurately. (If you have a particularly young group see the variation below.)

2   Now ask them if they know anything about the stories that the headlines refer to. It is not necessary (or possible) to go into great detail – this part of the exercise is simply to sensitise them to headlines.

3   Once you have done this, tell the students that they are going to make their own news stories. Put them into pairs and give each pair a copy of one of the headlines on photocopiable page 83.

4   Give the students five minutes to produce a list of the main points that they will include in their news story. They do not need to write sentences at this stage – just simple notes.

5   Go around the groups and get the general outline of their stories. Some of them may need a little prompting, and if any group is finding it really difficult to come up with anything, then give them a different headline.

6   Once they have the basic story, get each group to write their script. Tell them that it should be quite short (two minutes is the absolute maximum), but that they can use correspondents and reporters on site. In other words, one of them can be the anchor in the studio, and the other can be 'phoning in' a special report from the scene of the action.

7   Once they have written the script and rehearsed it, each segment can be recorded onto tape.

8   Each group now writes one question about their story for the others to answer as they listen. These questions can range from the simple (*How many people watched the race?*) to the complex (*What did our reporter suggest were the main problems with the concert?*) depending upon the level.

9   Students listen and answer their colleagues' questions.

Variation

1   For younger groups, talking about real headlines might not be appropriate. In this case, simply write three or four imaginary and fun headings on the board (possibly based on films e.g. *James Bond in Rome*) and ask them what they think the story behind them might be. Then proceed from Step 3.

2   You could do Step 2 with newspaper headlines or using the Internet – sites such as BBC (news.bbc.co.uk) or CNN (www.cnn.com). CNN also has streaming video which is updated every half hour for the most technologically advanced classes. (For more details see www.real.com)

MAN GROWS WINGS

NEW TEENAGE POLICE CREATED

MADONNA FOR PRESIDENT?

ARE ALIENS LIVING IN LONDON?

SPECIAL CONFERENCE IN MADRID

NEW FOOD DRUG DEVELOPED: NO NEED TO EAT ANY MORE!

SCANDAL FOR THE PRESIDENT

Big fight at concert

SCHOOL WAR BEGINS

GOVERNMENT WANTS ALL TEENAGERS TO WEAR UNIFORMS

THOUSANDS ESCAPE AS VOLCANO ERUPTS

Woman steals plane

NEW MOVIE – HUGE SUCCESS

We saw houses falling from the sky

MY CAT ATE MY HUSBAND

7 The restaurant

LEVEL: Elementary–intermediate

USING THIS PROJECT: This project is based around the idea that students create their own restaurant.

This project can be done over a few days, or spaced out over several weeks. It helps to bring in snacks and menus, especially for 7.2 and 7.3, to create the atmosphere of a real restaurant.

In addition, if possible, it is a great opportunity to tie a project in with extra-curricular activities such as a trip to a local restaurant to see how it works, a visiting speaker such as a local chef, a cooking competition or an international food party cooked by the students.

The final exercise (7.4) can be done in two ways – as a long or short activity. Because it is the culmination of the whole project, the longer version works better if 7.1, 7.2 and 7.3 have been done because students will have become involved in their restaurant and will want to see what happens to it.

	7.1 **Food families**	**7.2** **Setting up**	**7.3** **Dining out**	**7.4** **Our restaurant**
SKILLS	● speaking	● speaking ● writing	● speaking	● speaking ● reading
TIME	25–40 minutes	90 minutes	approx. 30 minutes	30 or 60 minutes
PREPARATION	● photocopying ● cutting ● finding examples of food	● collect logos ● photocopying	● preparing classroom (menus, numbers on tables, snacks) ● photocopying ● cutting	● photocopying ● cutting
CLASS SIZE	4 plus	3 plus	7–16	4 plus
PAGE NUMBER	86	88	90	92

Topic area
food, shopping, games

Language focus
Have you got ...?
(*Do you have ...?* in American English)
any
(alternative Step 6:
a/an vs. *some/any*)

Key vocabulary
shops: *butcher,
greengrocer,
off-licence, fishmonger*
food: *carrots, aubergines,
tomatoes, onions, pork,
beef, chicken, lamb, wine,
soft drinks, mineral water,
beer, cod, salmon, octopus,
prawns* and many others
as dictated by the class
rules: *dealer, face down*

Skills
speaking
(See page 15 for extra
activity on game play.)

Level
elementary–
intermediate

Time
25 minutes
(40 minutes if you do
the alternative in Step 6)

Materials
1 x set of cards on
page 87 per 4 students

7.1 Food families

Before class
1 Photocopy and cut up one set of cards and rules on page 87 per four students.

2 Possibly bring in some real vegetables, etc. to help explain difficult items.

In class
1 Make certain all the students are familiar with the language necessary for game play (see page 15).

2 Hold up the four 'people' cards from page 87 and make certain that students know what the four jobs are (greengrocer, butcher, fishmonger and off-licence owner).

3 Divide the class into groups of four and give each four a 'pack' of the cards from page 87, including the people cards and the food cards, but not the blank cards. Ask them to match the type of food with the person who sells it.

4 If there are insufficient students to make complete sets of four, have one or two smaller groups. Put the stronger students into this group as the task will be harder with fewer people.

5 When the groups have all finished mixing and matching, get feedback from the students and write on the board the lists of which food goes with which person.

6 Now hand out the four blank cards from page 87. Each member of each group draws an additional card for one of the shops (i.e. one person draws something extra from the greengrocer, one from the butcher, etc.). In each case, make certain that they check with you before they begin drawing. Have some spare blank cards ready just in case.
With stronger groups, simply hand out the people cards and get them to make up five different food cards themselves to match each person instead of giving them the prepared ones.

Note The cards show plural items so that all questions use the structure *Have you got any ...* except for the questions about people. However, if you decide to prepare your own cards this might be a good opportunity to revise singular/plural and countable/uncountable rules if the students draw a mixture of singular and plural items.

7 Once each group has finished ask them to swap their cards with another group and then to shuffle all the cards (hand-made and from this book) thoroughly.

8 Hand out the rules box from the next page.

9 At the end, gather together all of the hand-made cards and hold them up, making sure that all the students can identify them and putting a written record of what they are on the board.

Variation
In countries where mention of alcohol is inappropriate, change the *off-licence* to *supermarket* and make cards for *bread* and *rice*. If *pork* or *beef* are unacceptable, choose e.g. *duck* or a local speciality.

FAMILY CARDS

**Mr Grizzle
the Greengrocer**

**Mrs Baybon
the Butcher**

**Mr Fillit the
Fishmonger**

**Mrs Ambika the
Off-licence owner**

carrots 	aubergines 	tomatoes 	onions 
pork 	beef 	chicken 	lamb 
cod 	salmon 	prawns 	octopus 
wine 	soft drinks 	mineral water 	beer 

FOOD FAMILIES RULES

The aim of the game is to complete one family. This means one set of cards which are connected. The person who is collecting the grocer must get the grocer and the five food cards that go with him.

One person should be the dealer (the person who gives out the cards).

The dealer gives each person five cards, placing them face down on the table.

Organise your cards in your hand into families (i.e. the butcher with pork, beef, etc.).

Everybody looks at their cards and decides which family they are going to collect. Choose the family that you have most cards from.

The person on the dealer's right starts. He/She asks one other person (it doesn't matter who) the question *Have you got …?* (e.g. if you are collecting the grocer family, you might ask *Have you got any potatoes?* or *Have you got Mr Grizzle the Greengrocer?*)

The person must answer *Yes I have* or *No I haven't*. If they have, then they must give the card to the person who asked. After this or if the person has not got the card, the next person asks a question.

If you have given away all of your cards, then you can still ask other people for their cards.

When you think you have all the cards in a family, put them on the table. If you have got a whole family, you are the winner! If you have not, you must leave the game and give one card to each of the other players.

Topic area
food

Language focus
present simple

Key vocabulary
food / restaurant language
(e.g. *smoking/non-smoking, fried, boiled, grilled, sauce, marinated, dressing, light, chips, side dish, salad,* etc.) *courses* (see Step 5)

Skills
speaking
writing

Level
pre-intermediate
–intermediate

Time
90 minutes

Materials
famous logos
1 x page 89 per 4 students
pens or a word processor
(See page 13 for extra activity.)
paper for posters

7.2 Setting up

Before class
1   Collect a handful of well-known logos from magazines and products (e.g. the McDonald's 'M', the Shell shell, or the Nike logo, etc.).

2   Photocopy page 89 once per four students.

In class
1   Make sure that students are familiar with language connected with creating things (see page 15).

2   Show your students the logos and ask them to name the company that the symbol represents.

3   Put your students into groups of four or five. Tell them that they are going to open a restaurant and they need a name and a logo for it that people will remember. The name can be anything from a combination of their own names (the Joaroko, for example Joao and Hiroko) to the name of their favourite football team / TV show, etc. (the Manchester United Bar?). The logo that they create will be used throughout this activity (and throughout the whole project, if they do the following sections). It should be simple but fun.

4   Give them about 20 minutes to choose their name and design the logo. This stage is important because it helps them to believe in the company that they are creating.

5   Having completed their logo, each group now brainstorms the sort of food that they will serve. It should be a combination of foods from each country represented in the group. In a monolingual class, they can use food that they have heard of from different countries, or traditional dishes from different regions of their own. In certain cultures it will be necessary to pre-teach the idea of courses. Give a time limit of about 20 minutes for the brainstorming.

6   Once they have a list of food that they are going to sell, the students fill in the menu (photocopiable page 89), including the logo and the price, and a short description of what each meal is (e.g. FISH AND CHIPS – an English meal made from fried potatoes and fish). Explain that one pound equals one hundred pence, and compare the value of a pound with the value of the local currency. In addition, point out that we put the £ sign before the numerals rather than after (i.e. £1.45, not 1.45£).

7   Not all the students will be able to write on the menu at the same time, so the other students can make an A4 poster advertising the 'GRAND OPENING' of the restaurant. This should include the logo, a few drawings and little captions about the type of food offered, e.g. EXCELLENT VALUE FISH AND CHIPS. Students will rotate between Steps 6 and 7 until both are completed.

8   When everything has been finished, put together some tables and chairs and set up a 'restaurant', with the posters around the wall and the menus on each table (along with some crisps and drinks if you are feeling generous).

9   Each group can now visit the others' restaurants and see what they have on offer. They should check with the people who designed the menus if they don't understand what a dish is, and then choose their favourite dish from the other groups' restaurants.

Variation
In schools with computers, students can make a menu on screen. This gives students a change of environment and activity which stops the project becoming too classroom-bound.

Desserts

Drinks

Our address

-- fold here

Starters

Main Courses

-- fold here

PUT YOUR LOGO HERE

HOURS

Monday–Friday ....

Saturday ....

Sunday ....

MENU

by ....

Phone: ....

Fax: ....

E-mail: ....

Topic area
food, drama

Language focus
polite requests
complaints

Key vocabulary
phrases and questions
used in restaurants, e.g.
Could I have some …
Excuse me. What does
this mean? What would
you recommend? Where
are the toilets? Can I
have the bill, please.
high chair, to fire somebody

Skills
speaking (See page 17
for extra activity.)

Level
pre-intermediate–
intermediate

Time
c. 30 minutes depending
on level: a lower level
might take less time
while a higher level can
keep going longer

Materials
food and drink (snacks)
menus (original or
made from page 89)
1 x page 91 cut up
large number cards for
tables

7.3 Dining out

Before class
1 Prepare the classroom as a restaurant with menus (from local restaurants or from 7.2 Setting up, page 89), and with snacks (crisps, for example). In addition, each table will require a number card (1–7).

2 Photocopy, cut up and hand out the customer cards on page 91 (enough for one each).

3 Photocopy and cut up one set of waiter and manager cards on page 91.

4 **Optional** You might also like to make (or get the students to make) paper bow ties. Draw the shape of a bow tie on black paper, cut it out, make two holes and then thread string through it so that they can tie it round their necks.

In class
1 Make sure that students are familiar with language connected with speaking activities (see page 17).

2 Hand out the customer cards that you have cut up from page 91. If you have an odd number of students in your class, take one out of the group for a moment.

3 Each person starts calling out the line of dialogue on their card (ignoring the number, if they have one). At the same time they listen to try and find out who their partner is in the sequence (i.e. the line which makes sense when said either before or after theirs).

4 They must not stop calling out their line until they have found their partner. They must not show anybody their card.

5 When they have found their partner they sit down at their table (shown by the number at the end of the first card in each pair). For example, Student A has a card which says *Oh no. I have forgotten my wallet. Have you got any money?* with the number 6 at the end. He walks around caling it out until he finds his partner (Student B with *No, sorry I haven't.*), and then they go and sit at table 6.

6 The exceptions to this are the students who get the first two cards (with *W* and *M* in place of a number). The student who gets *You promised me more money. W* will become the waiter; the one with *M* is the manager.

7 If you have an odd number and have taken a student out at Step 2, now put him/her with group 5 and give him/her the line *No, I don't think so.*

8 Explain to the students that they are all in a restaurant and that their two (or three) lines represent the beginning of a conversation. They now have to think about who these people are, what they are talking about and what happens next. Give them about ten minutes in their pairs to work it out, and to devise small scenes beginning with the two lines. Finally, get willing students to act their 'mini-scenes' to the rest of the group.

9 Now give the waiter and the manager their respective cards from photocopiable page 91. Tell the students to keep doing their mini-scenes until the manager or waiter visits them, and then to interact with them.

10 The manager and waiter obey the commands on their cards and each story develops a little bit further, allowing them to make use of requests and complaints and also to create the busy atmosphere of a real restaurant.

11 As a final piece of feedback ask one member of each pair to describe exactly what happened when the manager or waiter approached them.

WAITER and MANAGER CARDS

a *Waiter*
The people on TABLE TWO have been complaining about the cold food. Tell them that they ordered chicken salad, and that you do not serve hot chicken in this restaurant.

d *Waiter*
Go to TABLE SEVEN and give them a key. Tell them that they left it in the restaurant last night.

g *Manager*
Go to TABLE SEVEN and tell them that they left their umbrella at the restaurant when they came for dinner last Wednesday.

b *Waiter*
You recognise your brother who is sitting at TABLE FOUR looking very unhappy. Go and ask him why he is sad.

e *Manager*
Go to TABLE ONE and politely ask the people there to be quiet. Some of the other people at tables near them are complaining about the noise.

h *Manager*
Fire the WAITER for making so many mistakes.

c *Waiter*
Go to TABLE FIVE and tell the customers that the chef has left and so the only food that they will be able to have is chicken salad or an omelette.

f *Manager*
Tell the people at TABLE THREE that their baby is too loud. (You do not like children.) There are no high chairs for babies in this restaurant.

i *Manager*
Take the bill to the people on TABLE SIX. You are in a hurry for them to leave because there are twenty people waiting for a table.

CUSTOMER CARDS

You promised me more money!

You must work harder. Maybe then I will give you more money!

We asked for a non-smoking table. That man is smoking!

I'm not going to ask him to stop.

This chicken is cold.

Yes. So is mine!

I told you that we shouldn't have brought the baby.

Perhaps the waiter can get us a high chair.

I brought you to this restaurant to give you some bad news

Oh no!

Is that the man over there?

I think so.

Oh no! I have forgotten my wallet. Have you got any money?

No. Sorry, I haven't.

I am afraid that I'm in love with another girl. I wanted to tell you yesterday but ...

Another girl? So that's where you were yesterday.

Our restaurant

Topic areas
work, food, maths

Language focus
hypothetical language, modals of possibility, decisions

Key vocabulary
food words (See 7.1.)
income, profit, loss, expenditure, poison, flood, protection money, burn, sack, staff, overheads

Skills
speaking
reading

Level
pre-intermediate +

Time
30–60 minutes

Materials
long version:
1 x page 93 per
4 students
short version:
1 x page 92 cut up per
4 students
dice
optional: calculators

Before class

1 Choose one of the two versions of this activity. The longer one takes one hour and the shorter one half an hour. The advantage of the longer version is that it provides a very real context for the students to work in, and therefore gives them a greater stake in the game. The shorter one is simpler and there are not so many numbers to worry about.

2 *Long version* Photocopy page 93 once per four students.

3 *Both versions* Photocopy and cut up one set of the cards on page 94 per four students.

In class

1 *Long version*
a) Put the students in groups of four (or two in smaller classes) and hand out a copy of page 93 to each group. They work through it, making decisions and filling in the gaps at each point. If they have done section 7.2 (page 88), the number of opening hours and average cost of meals will already have been worked out for the menu and they can use these figures. If not, they simply make them up, based on what is reasonable.
b) When it comes to the 'Outgoings' section, some of the figures are already filled in, and you may wish to set a minimum wage for the group to use in the wages section. The mathematics is much less important than the decision-making process and students anxious to make a lot of money by having lots of tables should note that this means they need more staff.
c) Allow the decision-making process to continue until each group has worked out their total profit (but no more than 15–20 minutes). This will be the significant figure for the game that follows.
Note You may wish to help and/or allow calculators at this stage to speed things up. Go to Step 3.

2 *Short version* Put the students in groups of four (or pairs in smaller classes). In this version, the students decide on the name of their restaurant and whether it is in the city or the countryside. You then tell each group that they make a profit of £7,000 per year. (Page 93 is therefore unnecessary.) Go to Step 3.

3 *Both versions* Explain to the students that they are now going to follow the progress of their restaurant over several years.

4 Give each group a copy of card number 1 from page 94 and a dice. Card number 1 says: *Your first year is a success. You get an extra £4,000. But Christmas is not good. Roll a dice to see how bad. 1, 2, 3: ask for card (5); 4, 5, 6: ask for card (15).* Each group, therefore, rolls the dice and asks you for the appropriate card. Each card links to another, sometimes by a dice roll, more often by the student being given two or three options. Emphasise at this stage that each group has to keep a running total as most cards will instruct them to either add or subtract quantities of money depending on their fortune (e.g. +£4,000 in the above example). Perhaps choose one member of each group to be the accountant.

5 Once the turn has finished each card has to be returned to you. You will then put that card back into the appropriate pile and give groups the next card that they ask for.

6 The winning group is not the first group to finish, but the group with the most money.

RESTAURANT FINANCES (long version only)

RESTAURANT NAME . . . .

LOCATION (City or countryside) . . . .

INCOME

NUMBER OF HOURS OPEN PER WEEK: . . . .

NUMBER OF TABLES: . . . .

AVERAGE COST OF MEALS: . . . .   £_____

WEEKLY INCOME: £_____
Each table has 1 meal every two hours with two people.
To work out your weekly income:
(number of tables x 2 x average cost of meals) x (number of hours open per week)

ANNUAL INCOME: £_____

Your weekly income x 52

EXPENDITURE

WAGES PER WEEK (for each person):   £_____

NUMBER OF STAFF: (you must have one for every 6 tables)

TOTAL WAGES PER YEAR: £_____
(The wages per week x number of staff x 52)

OVERHEADS: (lighting & electricity)   £2,000 per year

RENT   If your restaurant is in the country: £3,000 per year

         If your restaurant is in a town: £4,000 per year

FOOD TO BE COOKED: £700 per year per table

ANNUAL EXPENDITURE: £_____
Rent+Overheads+Food+Total Wages per Year

PROFIT   £_____
Annual income – annual expenditure

Restaurant Choice Cards

4 The pop stars you invited to the party destroy all your furniture and burn your kitchen. Roll the dice. You lose that amount × £1,000. You must close the restaurant for a month. Go to (**9**).

8 There is a bomb in the city centre. The restaurant is OK, but many guests do not want to eat there. You lose £1,000. Do you move your restaurant to the country (**2**) or offer free meals for teenagers (**11**)?

12 END OF THE YEAR. It was a bad year for you. This year you only made half of last year's profits (add half your profit to your total). If your restaurant is in the city go to (**8**), if it is in the country go to (**2**).

16 You refuse to pay the Mafia. They set fire to your restaurant. You stop the fire before the worst, but it costs £8,000 to repair. When they come back, do you pay (**17**) or call the police (**18**)?

20 The change of name was a bad idea. Your restaurant loses many customers and all your staff leave you. Change the name back to the original name and go to (**24**).

24 Your restaurant begins to do well again. You get £3,000 this month. Do you spend it on your restaurant (**14**), make your meals cheaper (**23**) or pay your chef more money (**19**)?

3 You open a new quality restaurant. It costs you £25,000. You can have a party to increase profits (**4**) or move the restaurant into the city centre (**8**).

7 You open a restaurant selling only hamburgers. You make £4,000, but then things go wrong: you lose £2,400. Do you close the restaurant and open a quality restaurant (**3**) or have a big party with some pop star friends of yours (**4**)?

11 The teenage meals are a great success. You open a night-club downstairs as well. Roll the dice. You earn this × £2,000. Do you do nothing (**10**) or change the name to WILD BAR (**20**)?

15 Everything gets worse and worse. Your restaurant closes and you lose all your money. But … you decide to try again (go back to **1**).

19 The chef is very happy and cooks lots of good food. You make £900 extra in a week. You can open a new restaurant (**22**) or go on a long holiday (**12**).

23 END OF THE YEAR! Add your PROFIT to your total. Do you expand your restaurant (**14**), start selling only hamburgers (**7**) or have a party with your favourite pop stars (**4**)?

2 There are terrible storms in the countryside and your restaurant is flooded. Do you close the restaurant for a month (**9**) or stay open in the rain (**15**)?

6 The new chef is a disaster. He cannot cook anything! You lose £2,000 business in one month. He says his salary is too low. You can sack him (**23**) or pay him more (**19**).

10 Two Mafia men appear at your door. They want protection money. Do you pay (**13**), refuse to pay (**16**) or call the police (**18**)?

14 You expand your restaurant but something goes wrong. Some of your customers get food poisoning. Roll the dice – you lose that amount × £500. Go to (**24**).

18 You call the police. They take away the criminals and you receive a huge reward: £12,000. Your restaurant becomes famous because of this. Do you change the name to THE FAMOUS CRIME RESTAURANT (**20**) or not (**21**)?

22 You open a new restaurant near your old one. It costs you £15,000 to open. You can either sell only hamburgers (**7**) or quality food (**3**).

1 Your first year is a success. You get an extra £4,000. But Christmas is not good. Roll a dice to see how bad. 1, 2, 3: ask for card (**5**); 4, 5, 6: ask for card (**15**).

5 You get a bad review in the local newspaper and lose some business (you lose £3,500). Either: get a new chef (**6**) or ignore the newspaper (**24**).

9 You re-open your restaurant. Do you employ a new chef (**6**) or keep the old one (**10**)?

13 You pay the money (£1,000) and they come back. Then, you pay £1,500. They come back. Now they want even more. Do you pay them (**17**), refuse to pay (**16**) or call the police (**18**)?

17 You pay the Mafia £2,000. Now they want £5,000 a month and free meals! Do you refuse to pay (**16**) or call the police (**18**)?

21 SUCCESS!!! Your restaurant is a great success around the world. Add your PROFIT to your total, and see how much money you have made.

From *Imaginative Projects* by Matt Wicks © Cambridge University Press 2000 **PHOTOCOPIABLE**

8 Secret agent

LEVEL: Pre-intermediate–upper-intermediate

USING THIS PROJECT: This is a narrative project in which students become secret agents. First they prepare their cars with gadgets and devices (8.1); then they are sent to investigate the disappearance of fellow agent, Moira Copter. They receive a coded message (8.2) which directs them to Dr Drakken in Cambridge. When they arrive there, Dr Drakken has been murdered (8.3) and they must interrogate a number of local witnesses. This leads them to the information that Moira Copter has been kidnapped by the Rooster, an international terrorist who is hiding in his base in Brazil. They must get into the base to rescue Moira (8.4).

The project provides all sorts of opportunities for bringing in films, pictures, even toys that teenagers had when they were younger, with which to create a sense of the world of a secret agent.

Generally speaking, because of the narrative thrust of this project, it is better done over a short period of time so that students are involved in the story without letting it continue too long.

	8.1 **Equipping your agent**	**8.2** **Codes**	**8.3** **Interrogation**	**8.4** **The base**
SKILLS	• speaking • writing	• speaking • writing	• reading • speaking	• speaking
TIME	60 minutes	45 minutes	60 minutes	55 minutes
PREPARATION	• photocopying • cutting up	• photocopying • cutting up	• photocopying • cutting up	• photocopying • cutting up • optional: writing cards appropriate for your group
CLASS SIZE	4 plus	2 plus	6 plus	4 plus
PAGE NUMBER	96	98	100	103

8.1 Equipping your agent

Topic areas
cars, spies, people, art

Language focus
spatial prepositions
present simple
modals of ability
passive
is used to/for ...

Key vocabulary
gadget, acid, bullet proof,
machine guns
words on cards on
page 97

Skills
speaking
writing

Level
pre-intermediate–
upper-intermediate

Time
60 minutes

Materials
I cut up x page 97 per
student
pens
paper
card (to mount
pictures)
(See page 13 for extra
activity on creating
things.)
optional: clip from
James Bond film

Before class

1 Photocopy and cut up each one of sections A, B and C on page 97 per student.

2 Gather cards, pens, paper and glue. In addition, if you do not wish the students to draw (Step 11) then you will need to find substitute photos of cars.

In class

1 Make sure that your students are familiar with the appropriate classroom language for the exercise. (See page 13.)

2 To pre-teach car vocabulary, hand out copies of section A of photocopiable page 97 and tell your students that they are secret agents and this is their car.

3 Give them copies of the labels from section B and ask them to fit these labels to the appropriate part of the car. Alternatively, this can be done as a whole-class activity if the picture of the car is enlarged and two or three copies are pinned up around the room. The students are then given the section B cards which they race to glue / pin on.

4 Once the students have completed the diagram, ask them to explain what certain parts are used for.

5 Write a sample sentence on the board using the structure *is used to / for.* (e.g. *The indicators are used to show where we are going.*)

6 Write the following parts on the board: *headlights, windscreen, windscreen wipers, steering wheel* and *seats.* Ask the students to make sentences in pairs explaining what each of these parts of the car is used for.

7 The class report back. You could write a couple more sentences on the board so that students have a clear written record.

8 Remind your students that they are secret agents and tell them that another secret agent – Moira Copter – has been kidnapped, and that they have been approached by the EIA (English Intelligence Agency) to rescue her. In order to do that, their car will be fitted with all the latest gadgets.

9 Put the students in pairs or threes. Give them some paper and pens to draw a car with. They can model their drawings on a real car or an imaginary one. If they really can't draw, or if you prefer, they could use a photograph of a car from an advert and simply glue it onto their paper.

10 Now they have to imagine what gadgets are going to be added to their car: machine guns from the lights, perhaps? An oil slick from the exhaust pipe? You can offer non-violent suggestions, such as heavily scented flowers bursting from the boot in order to confuse the enemy. Once they have decided on five or six things that they are going to include, they can then label their diagram as in the example in section C of photocopiable page 97. Draw their attention to the use of the structure of *is used to / for* and encourage them to use it where possible.

11 Finally, each group should present the results of their work to the rest of the group. They are, effectively, in the position of 'Q' in the James Bond films, having to explain to their colleagues what modifications they have made and how each one will work. This exercise can be repeated or extended for other equipment for those who finish too quickly: the agent's briefcase, gun, helicopter, motorbike, etc.

Now they are ready for the mission ...

THE AGENT'S CAR

Section A

Section B

body	bonnet	pedals
wheel	boot	roof
headlights	exhaust pipe	seats
indicator	number plate	wing mirrors
windscreen	dashboard	door
windscreen wiper	steering wheel	

Section C

The windscreen is bullet proof.

The bonnet is electrified.

The number plate is used to hide two machine guns.

The wheels are used to cut other cars' wheels.

The headlights are used to fire acid at other cars.

8.2 Codes

Topic areas
spies, people

Language focus
letters/alphabet
recent vocabulary

Key vocabulary
sharks, briefcase, ransom,
to break a code
optional: car vocabulary
from 8.1 (See Step 7.)

Skills
speaking
writing

Level
pre-intermediate –
upper-intermediate

Time
45 minutes

Materials
1 x section A page 99
per pair
1 x section B page 99
per pair
1 x section C page 99
per student
pens

Before class

1   Photocopy and cut up one set of section A page 99 for half the students in your class and one set of section B on the same page for the other half.

2   If you do Step 7, photocopy and cut up one set of section C on page 99 for each student.

In class

1   Divide the class into pairs. In each pair, one student receives the A part of photocopiable page 99 and one the B part.

2   Tell them that they are secret agents and that they received these messages from their headquarters this morning – they must be decoded quickly.

3   The students should be able to decipher their respective coded messages using the information in the CODE BOX. They can work out the letters that are missing by comparing words and sharing the information that they each have. (Note that the letters on the left side of the CODE BOX refer to the coded alphabet, those on the right to the real alphabet.)

4   Give about ten minutes to decode the messages. Students then read their answers back to you. A students should have: 'I will feed Moira Copter to the sharks if you do not give me ten million pounds. Reply in code.' Bs should get: 'Leave the money in a briefcase at ten o'clock tomorrow. Tell me in code where you will leave it.' Put together, they explain the problem: Moira Copter (a colleague) has been kidnapped and they have to pay a ransom.

5   Now the students write a short reply to the criminals in code (using the code from Step 4). (I will never pay! would be written G EGNN KYDYB MPU!)

6   Having finished they should give their coded message to another pair to check and decode. This should take about five minutes.

7   *Optional*
a) Tell the students that their commander has just sent them further instructions. This time, however, it is in a different code: the RV code system (Recent Vocabulary). The code is simply written with recent vocabulary in the middle of each word, so that HAPCARPY = HAPPY + CAR.
b) Give the students the message in section C of page 99. This code is based on transport vocabulary (as in 8.1 on page 96), but the message could easily be rewritten with something more relevant to your group. With a weaker class, you may write the list of recent vocabulary on the board.
c) The message in section C reads: Moira is a prisoner of the rooster. Doctor Drakken in Cambridge knows where his secret base is.
d) The text actually reads as follows:
MODASHBOARDIRAISLIGHTSAPRWINDSCREENISONEROMIRRORFTHEXHAUSTE
ROOSSEATTERDOCTBONNETORDRABOOTKKENIINDICATORNCAMBSEATBELRIDGEKN
OCARWSWHEWHEELREHBRAKEISBASEIROOFS.

Therefore, the words are: dashboard, lights, windscreen, mirror, exhaust, seat, bonnet, boot, indicator, seat belt, car, wheel, brake, roof.

e) Encourage the students to treat the exercise like a word search in order to solve the mystery.

Code answers: CODE = real
A=q B=r C=s D=v E=w F=x G=i H=j I=k J=m K=n L=o M=p
N=l O=h P=a Q=b R=c S=f T=u U=y V=z W=t X=d Y=e Z=g

CODE PAGE

SECTION A

Help your partner break the code.

G EGNN SYYX JLGBP RLMWYB

WL WOY COPBIC GS ULT XL

KLW ZGDY JY WYK JGNNGLK

MLTKXC. BYMNU GK RLXY.

CODE BOX

CODE = real
N=l Y=e R=c W=t C=s
J=m O=h I=k S=f
T=   Q=   P=

SECTION B

Help your partner break the code.

NYPDY WOY JLKYU GK

P QBGYSRPCY PW WYK L RNLRI

WLJLBBLE. WYNN JY GK RLXY

EOYBY ULT EGNN NYPDY GW.

CODE BOX

CODE = real
G=i E=w B=r U=y X=d
D=v K=n M=p Y=e
L=   Z=

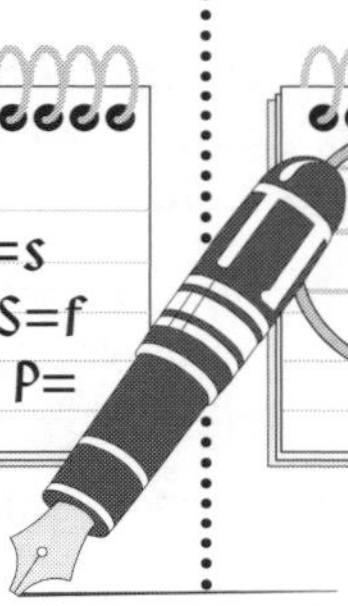

SECTION C

THIS IS AN URGENT MESSAGE FROM THE COMMANDER TO AGENT ENGLISH 1:

MODASHBOARDIRAISLIGHTSAPRWIND
SCREENISONEROMIRRORFTHEXHAUS
TEROOSSEATTERDOCTBONNETORDRA
BOOTKKENIINDICATORNCAMBSEAT
BELTRIDGEKNOCARWSWHEWHEELRE
HBRAKEISBASEIROOFS.

Topic areas
spies, people, crime, drama

Language focus
question forms / indirect questions
simple past
past continuous
present perfect

Key vocabulary
investigate, interrogate, fingerprints, gang, thug, kidnap, alibi, witness, suspect, agitated, addict, mad, find out

Skills
reading
speaking

Level
pre-intermediate–upper-intermediate

Time
60 minutes (but see also Step 9)

Materials
1 x page 101 per student
1 x cut up page 102 per class (with additional card 10s if required)
item for passing around (Step 13)

8.3 Interrogation

Before class

1 Photocopy one page 101 per student. Cut off the question section.

2 Photocopy and cut up the cards on page 102. Each student should have one card. If you have more than ten students, then copy card 10 several times.

In class

1 Hand out a copy of the newspaper story from page 101 to each student.

2 Divide the class into groups of three or four and get them to do a reading race using the questions from page 101 to check that they have understood the text. (For details of how to do a reading race see 3.2 page 44.)

3 Now tell your class that they are secret agents who are going to try and find out who murdered Dr Drakken and what happened to Moira Copter. Check that they know the meanings of all the words on the role cards on photocopiable page 102.

4 Divide the class up into *witnesses* and *interrogators*. Approximately one third of the class should be interrogators, and the rest witnesses. If you need more than ten witnesses, give out extra copies of card 10 (the 'Thug'), which means that the Rooster sent more than one thug to Cambridge. If you have fewer than ten witnesses start at number 1 and use the cards consecutively (i.e. for four witnesses use cards 1, 2, 3 and 4). Whatever happens, you will need a minimum of two interrogators and four witnesses.

5 The interrogators think of questions to ask the witnesses. Encourage them to phrase the questions correctly differentiating between the present perfect (*How long have you known X?*) and the past continuous (*What were you doing at 7.30 last night?*).

6 The witnesses, meanwhile, read their role cards and make certain that they agree on their various alibis (wherever possible). Give the students about fifteen minutes for this part of the activity. They must not show their cards to the interrogators.

7 When the students have completed their preparation, bring the two groups together and re-divide them. Start the interrogations. Each interrogator takes one or more witnesses. They should go to one side. Interrogations work best if witnesses don't hear each other, so the witnesses who are waiting to be interviewed should stay in their groups, preparing their stories. In a small class the two interrogators deal with half the class each. In a larger class, each interrogator will have fewer witnesses.

8 Once the interrogations have been completed (after about ten minutes) the class returns to the original groups.

9 The interrogators compare notes and see if they can come up with a solution, while the witnesses recount their experiences to each other to make certain they have not contradicted each other's stories.

10 Then, as a whole-class activity, the interrogators go to one side of the room and the witnesses to the other. This time, any interrogator may cross-question any witness. To control this, have an object, such as a pencil case, which is passed around. Only the interrogator holding the object may speak. They must pass it on regularly to other interrogators.

11 Finally, once all questions have been completed, the interrogators accuse one of the witnesses of being the murderer. If they are right, the interrogators' team wins. If not, then the witnesses win.

NEWSPAPER INFORMATION PAGE

NEW ENGLISH TIMES

Volume 1 Issue 123   08 November 2012   £3

INSIDE THIS ISSUE

Dr Drakken	2
Your stars	2
New films	2
New football rules	3
All schools to close	4
Madonna Interview	5
Financial Reports	6

THE WEATHER

There will be rain from the north heading towards the south.
In southern areas there will be more rain. The outlook for the next two weeks is rain every day, with some snow at the weekend.

MAN FOUND DEAD IN LONDON ROAD

Last night, at about 7p.m., the body of Dr Francis Drakken was found in London Road, Cambridge. He had been shot six times.

Dr Francis Drakken was a famous engineer working for the English Intelligence Agency. At the time of his death, he was investigating a kidnapping. Police have several witnesses to interrogate about the murder.

Dr Drakken was born in 1956 in Oxford. He had three children and had been working with his assistant, Marcus Perolius, for many years.

Dr Drakken was investigating the disappearance of Moira Copter, the rich and beautiful daughter of Professor Heli Copter, whose factory she was working at when she was kidnapped six days ago.

The gun used to kill Dr Drakken was found in the River Cam near the city centre, but there were no fingerprints on it.

Police think that the Rooster – a famous international criminal – and his gang might have been involved in the murder.

There is some confusion about where some witnesses were at the time of the murder:

Marcus Perolius claims that he was in the *Eagle* Restaurant with his girlfriend, Lucinda Lovealot.

However, a man called Tony says that he was at the cinema, watching *Titanic II* with Lucinda.

Lucinda's husband says that he was playing golf at the time of the murder, but promises that if he ever sees Marcus Perolius or Tony again he will kill them both.

Police are also speaking to Professor Heli Copter who was supposed to have a meeting with Dr Drakken at 7.30 about his missing daughter, Moira.

QUESTIONS

1. Who was killed?
2. Who did Dr Francis Drakken work for?
3. Who is Moira Copter?
4. What has happened to Moira Copter?
5. Who is the Rooster?
6. Where was Marcus Perolius when the murder was committed?
7. Who was watching *Titanic II*?
8. Who was supposed to meet Dr Drakken at 7.30 p.m.?

ROLE CARDS FOR WITNESSES

1 You are Dr Drakken's assistant, Marcus Perolius. You murdered Dr Drakken because he discovered that the Rooster – your real boss – had kidnapped Moira Copter and taken her to his headquarters in Brazil.

2 You are Lucinda Lovealot. You are Marcus Perolius' girlfriend. On the night of the murder you were selling drugs in the city centre. Marcus asked you to tell a lie and say that you were both in the *Eagle* restaurant.

3 You are Bob Dicap, the owner of the *Eagle* restaurant. Last night was very busy, but you cannot remember seeing Lovealot or Perolius.

4 You are a waiter at the *Eagle* restaurant. You are a drug addict. Lovealot has said that she will give you £1,000,000 if you lie and say that you saw her and her boyfriend Marcus Perolius in the restaurant last night.

5 You are a business colleague of Marcus Perolius. Last night at 6.30 you saw Marcus hurrying back to his factory. Normally, he stops and talks to you, but last night he was very agitated.

6 Your name is Tony and you are mad. You have been in love with Lucinda Lovealot for many years. You believe that you went to the cinema with her last night (although you did not!).

7 You are Professor Heli Copter. You were supposed to have a meeting with Dr Drakken last night at 7.30 p.m. He said that he had some information about your missing daughter, Moira.

8 You are Lucinda Lovealot's husband, and you are a very jealous man. Last night you were playing golf with your friends.

9 You work at the cinema and you cannot see very well. Last night, during the film *Titanic II*, you thought you saw your brother Tony with a woman.

10 You are a thug and you work for the Rooster, an international criminal. Last night you went to kill Dr Drakken because he had found out too much information about your boss – but you were too late. By the time you arrived he was already dead!

8.4 The base

Topic areas
spies, crime, games

Language focus
question forms
instructions
recent vocabulary
word order

Key vocabulary
trap, shortcut, mime,
corridor
depends on the cards
used in the game (see
Step 4)
(See page 15 for
additional activity on
game play.)

Skills
speaking

Level
intermediate (using the
cards in this book)
any level (if you adapt
the trap cards)

Time
30 minutes (making the
traps)
25 minutes (playing the
game)

Materials
1 x page 104 per 4
students
1 x cut up page 105 per
student
stopwatch/watch
1 dice per 4 students
counters

Before class

1   Photocopy page 104 once per four students.

2   Photocopy and cut up one set of cards on page 105 per student.

In class

1   Ensure that the students know the language for game play (see page 15.)

2   Divide the class into two groups, A and B. Tell them that they are secret agents and that a colleague of theirs, Moira Copter, has been kidnapped and taken to Brazil by the international criminal known as the Rooster. They have to rescue her by getting into the Rooster's headquarters.

3   Show them the game board (page 104) and explain that they have to get from start to finish and avoid the traps on the way. Before they begin playing, however, they must create the traps for the other group.

4   Give each student a copy of the ten cut up cards (from page 105). Explain that each card corresponds to one trap on the map.

5   Ask a student to read the first card aloud. *Think of three words that you have learnt recently. Now change the order of the letters to make an anagram. e.g. RABBIT = BARTIB.* The students then make up their own anagram in groups. (To teach this, get them to make anagrams of their own names – Matt Wicks, for example, becomes, Twam Stick; Maria could be Airam.) (The other instructions on the card, *When the other group lands on this trap they have 2 minutes to work out what the 3 words are* are only used during the actual game.)

6   Each group should then make up the three anagrams for trap one, keeping their words secret from the other group. Each student in the group needs to keep a record of the traps. They do the same for the other traps / cards. This stage could be done as homework to reduce the amount of class time needed.

7   When the traps are all ready, re-divide the class, putting two As with two Bs.

8   The students are now ready to play. They play in fours (i.e. two As against two Bs). Either read out or photocopy the RULES BOX below. Demonstrate what happens when a student lands on a *Trap* square (i.e. the opposing team reads out the 'during the game' section of the appropriate *Trap card*).

RULES
Each team puts a counter (a coin or a small object) on *square 1*.
Both teams roll the dice. The highest scorer begins.
Roll the dice again. You can move the number of spaces you roll.
You cannot pass over a *trap square*. You must land on it. If you are on square 13, for example, and you throw a 4, you can only move two spaces because you must stop at the trap.

When you land on a *trap square* then the other side will read you a card telling you what to do.

If you answer the question on the *trap square* correctly then you can move again next turn. If not, then you have to try the trap again until you get it right.

The last square (40) contains Moira Copter. To free her and win the game you must throw exactly the right number. (If you are on number 38 you must throw a 2. If you are on number 36 you must throw a 4, etc.)

THE BASE BOARD

START

1 THE SEA

2 THE SEA Go forward one space.

3 TRAP ONE REMEMBER! STOP AT THE TRAP.

4 YOU SEE A SHORTCUT. Go forward 3.

5 THE JUNGLE Go back 2.

10

9 THE ROAD TO THE HEAD-QUARTERS

8 A LOCAL VILLAGER HELPS YOU. Go forward 2.

7 TRAP TWO

6

11 TRAP THREE

12 Ssssh! Guard sleeping. Miss a turn.

13 RECEPTION

14 RECEPTION Go forward 1.

15 TRAP FOUR

16 DINING ROOM

17

22 ALARM! Go back to square 17.

21 CORRIDOR Go back 3.

20 CORRIDOR Go back 1.

19 TRAP FIVE

18

23 WEAPONS ROOM

24 EXPLOSION! Go back to the entrance.

25 WEAPONS ROOM

26 SECRET DOOR Go forward 3.

27 TRAP SIX

28 DARK TUNNEL Miss a turn.

29 TRAP SEVEN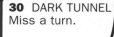

30 DARK TUNNEL Miss a turn.

34 CONTROL ROOM

33 THE ELEVATOR EXPLODES. Go back 7 spaces.

32 TRAP EIGHT

31

35 CONTROL ROOM Miss a turn.

36 GUARDS ATTACK YOU. Go back 4 spaces.

37 TRAP NINE

38

39 TRAP TEN

40 MISSION SUCCESSFUL What took you so long?

FINISH

TRAP CARDS

TRAP ONE
Before the game:
Think of 3 words that you have learnt recently. Now change the order of the letters to make an anagram. (e.g. RABBIT=BARTIB).
During the game [square 3]:
When the other group lands on this square read them your anagram (spell it out for them). They have 2 minutes to work out what the 3 words are.

TRAP TWO
Before the game:
Write 3 sentences. Now change them so that each one has one grammar mistake.
(e.g. She was working as a teacher. = She was working a teacher.)
During the game [square 7]:
When the other group lands on this square they have 2 minutes to find the mistakes in your sentences and correct them.

TRAP THREE
Before the game:
Think of 3 words that you have learnt recently. Write the definitions.
(e.g. You can see through this on a car.)
During the game [square 11]:
When the other group lands on this square read them your definitions. They have 2 minutes to guess each word.
(e.g. window)

TRAP FOUR
Before the game:
Write 2 sentences. Then change the order of the words.
(e.g. The train is going to arrive at about 8 p.m. = about is train going arrive the to p.m. at 8)
During the game [square 15]:
When the other group lands on this square they have 2 minutes to put the sentences in the correct order.

TRAP FIVE
Before the game:
Choose 3 words that you have learnt recently.
During the game [square 19]:
When the group lands on this trap tell them your words. They then have 2 minutes to make a sentence for each word.

TRAP SIX
Before the game:
Think of 3 words that you think are difficult to pronounce. Now make a sentence for each word.
During the game [square 27]:
When the opposite group lands on this trap they have to read your sentences (and pronounce them well!).

TRAP SEVEN
Before the game:
Think of 3 words that you always find difficult to spell.
During the game [square 29]:
When the other group lands on this trap they have to spell the words you tell them. They are not allowed to make any mistakes! They have 2 minutes to do this.

TRAP EIGHT
Before the game:
Write 3 questions. Now change the order of the words around.
(e.g. Where is your beautiful jumper from? = jumper beautiful where from is your?)
During the game [square 32]:
When the other group lands on this trap they have to reorganise the words into the correct order. They have 2 minutes to do this.

TRAP NINE
Before the game:
Think of 2 rooms in a house.
(e.g. kitchen, dining room)
During the game [square 37]:
When the other group lands on this trap, they must think of 6 things that can be found in each room that you name. They have 2 minutes to do this.

TRAP TEN
Before the game:
Think of 3 things that you wish you could do.
(e.g. I wish I could go to the beach now.)
During the game [square 39]:
When the other group lands on this trap you have to mime your 3 wishes and they must guess what you are miming – using grammatically correct sentences.

Some students in Portugal performing 'A midsummer night's project'

9 A midsummer night's project

LEVEL: intermediate or mixed-ability class

USING THIS PROJECT: Note that this project is designed to be done as a complete item and cannot be easily broken down into mini-projects. This means that, while items may be added or omitted, in general the project should be followed through. The script for this project has been (liberally) adapted from William Shakespeare's *A Midsummer Night's Dream* and provides a range of activities for students of different levels. Ideally, it should be done with a class of intermediate students or above. Alternatively, it can be done with a mixed-ability group (at the end of term, perhaps) with the weaker students taking on the easier roles. There is also the possibility of work on set design, costumes and masks.

If possible, video the performance. Students always want to see themselves, and it is great to watch a few months later and see how their English has improved. It can also be useful for motivating the next group. Proud parents always want a copy too.

Note that timings are very approximate as there are many ways of doing the play, with a number of extra optional activities. The times given are based on an average production, but the number / level of students will cause times to vary.

	9.1 Introduction and background	**9.2 Auditions**	**9.3 Rehearsals and preparation**	**9.4 The performance**
SKILLS	• speaking • listening	• reading • speaking	• speaking • reading • writing • listening	• speaking • writing
TIME	20 minutes	2½–4 hours	approx. 10 hours*	each performance: 25 minutes
PREPARATION	• none	• photocopying	• photocopying • cutting out • optional: finding coloured paper, toilet rolls, etc. • bringing songs	• completing 9.3
CLASS SIZE	10–25	10–25	10–25	10–25
PAGE NUMBER	108	109	110	112

9.1 Introduction and background

Topic area
famous people, media, theatre

Language focus
past simple
past perfect
descriptions

Key vocabulary
birthday (lower level),
dream, midsummer

Skills
speaking
listening

Level
intermediate or
a mixed-ability class

Time
20 minutes

Materials
optional: picture of
William Shakespeare

In class

1 Elicit from your students who William Shakespeare was. Ideally, this should be done by holding up a picture of him, which can be found in any good encyclopaedia or on the Internet at http://www.stratford-upon-avon.co.uk/. Ask what they know about him and write it on the board.

2 Divide the class into two teams and tell them that you are going to read them eight sentences about William Shakespeare. They should write down on a piece of paper (one piece per team) whether they think each sentence is true or false.

3 Read out the sentences:

> a) William Shakespeare was born in Bradford-on-Avon.
> b) Shakespeare died on his birthday.
> c) He was born in 1564.
> d) He wrote 36 plays.
> e) One of his plays was called *Hamnet*.
> f) One of his plays was called *A Midsummer Night's Dream*.
> g) He lived most of his life in London.
> h) In his play, *Romeo and Juliet*, Romeo and Juliet were brother and sister.

4 Collect in the papers and check them, or give them to the opposing team to check. Go through the answers as you do so.

> a) False. He was born in *Stratford*-on-Avon.
> b) True, he died on April 23rd 1616 and was born on April 23rd 1564.
> c) True.
> d) Well, yes. He actually wrote more, but only 36 survive.
> e) False. His son was called Hamnet. One of his plays was called *Hamlet*.
> f) True. Elicit from the students what they think it means from the title (a dream in the middle of summer!).
> g) True. And most of his plays were performed at the Globe Theatre which has recently been rebuilt (more information on the Internet at: http://www.shakespeares-globe.org/)
> h) False. They were in love.

5 Now tell the students that they are going to have an opportunity to put on a production of *A Midsummer Night's Dream*.

9.2 Auditions

Topic area
famous people, stories, theatre, drama

Language focus
direct speech

Key vocabulary
duke, palace, sword, fairy, mischief, cruel, execute, chewing gum, sweetheart, carrot, silly, behind-the-scenes

Skills
reading
speaking

Level
intermediate or
a mixed-ability class

Time
Introductory section:
90 minutes (if play is read in one lesson)
3 hours (if play is read over several lessons)
Auditions:
60 minutes approx.
(depending on the number of people in your class)

Materials
photocopy 1 x pages
113–116 per person

Before class

1   Look at the script on pages 113–116. You will notice that some gaps have been left. These are for you and/or students to fill in with local references, to make the text funnier and more personal to each group.

2   Once you have filled in these lines, photocopy enough scripts for everyone in the class to have one each.

In class

(A) Handing out the script

1   If you have time, hand out the script at the rate of one scene per day, reading it aloud in class and then doing one of the follow-up activities suggested below.

2   If there is insufficient time, hand out the script in one go, and get the students to read it aloud. Then choose one of the follow-up activities below to do.

Follow up

*   A wall poster/chronology showing the main events: This can be done as a whole after the play has been read once or twice, or done daily and added to as each new scene is revealed.

*   Prediction activities: What do you think will happen to Helena / Hermia in the next scene? Write these down on a piece of paper and compare them with what happens when the next scene is read the following day. Alternatively, if you are reading the play as a whole rather than day-by-day, then stop after each scene, elicit ideas and write them on the board.

*   Adjective posters: Students draw a picture of each character on the first day and surround the character with thought bubbles containing appropriate adjectives, adding more each day as they read further scenes. Alternatively, they can make one poster after reading the whole play rather than doing it scene-by-scene.

(B) Casting: procedure
There are two approaches to casting the play, and in the end the nature of the group and the amount of time available will dictate which one you choose.

*   Ask the students who wants to act and who wants to work 'behind-the-scenes'. Give roles to the actors and responsibilities to the behind-the-scenes people (sets, costumes, props and sound). This is quick and efficient.

*   Alternatively, get the students who want to work behind-the-scenes to select their own responsibilities (as long as everything is covered). Then, audition the actors for the roles. Tell them that they can read any role that they want and the group can have a secret ballot to decide who gets which role, based on who is the most suitable for the part. This is fun and adds an extra activity to the project. However, sensitivity needs to be shown in choosing students of varied levels and abilities.

Variation

Small classes can reduce the number of actors needed by doubling up the role of Narrator and another character, as well as making Oberon and Theseus the same actor. In addition, students with smaller parts will need to be involved in the behind-the-scenes work or there will be nothing for them to do at certain points. Give out their responsibilities at this stage as well.

9.3 Rehearsals and preparation

Topic area
media, theatre

Language focus
instructions
direct speech

Key vocabulary
duke, palace, sword, fairy,
mischief, cruel, execute,
chewing gum, sweetheart,
carrot, silly, wand, mask

Skills
speaking (See page 17.)
reading
writing
listening

Level
intermediate or a
mixed-ability class

Time
10 hours approx.
depending on the size of
the class and scale of the
production
Note Activities A–D are
done at the same time
as each other.

Before class
(Activities A and B)

1 Complete 9.1 and 9.2.

2 Check that students are familiar with the language practised in the extra activities on pages 13 and 17.

3 Collect materials for building the set, for example card, toilet rolls, silver foil, glue, scissors and sellotape.

In class

Activity A: Rehearsing

Rehearsal for the show can take a variety of forms:

* Students can read the lines, and you provide error correction and intonation work.

* Students can read the lines, exaggerating a particular emotion. For example, when *Hermia* says 'Oh, Lysander, please stop. I am so tired', she is exhausted. To emphasise this, get Hermia to stress *please* and *so* melodramatically. You can drill a line like this with the whole class because it is useful stress and intonation practice.

* Students can get up and walk around with an appointed director for each scene to tell them where to move to. Remind them not to have their backs to the audience.

* Students can improvise a scene. Remove the script and just let them act as the characters. For example, what would happen if Lysander and Helena had dinner together? Everybody in the class works in pairs to invent their own scenes.

Activity B: The set

The set design can be simple or complex, depending on the class.

* *Simple version:* Students take the biggest piece of paper they can find and draw two pictures – one of a palace and one of a forest. At the beginning of the play, they pin up the palace behind the actors and at the end of scene I, they change this for the picture of the forest.

* *Complex version:* Students build trees by using the insides of toilet / kitchen rolls covered with coloured paper, to make the trunks. They cut out fairly big leaves and staple them onto the top of the trunks.

* In both cases, you will need to make a throne by covering a chair with tin foil. This makes it look as if it is made from silver – although Theseus has to be careful sitting on it.

   Remember – students often have the best ideas for these things.

9.3 **Rehearsals and preparation** (continued)

Materials

A: photocopy 1 x page 113 – 116 per student
B: various props (see text)
optional: toilet rolls, coloured card, scissors, paints, foil and other art materials
optional: popular songs (See Additional activity.)
C: old clothes, art materials (for making the donkey mask)
D: cardboard, glue, glitter, sequins, coloured pens, alarm clock

Before class

(Activities C and D)

1 Complete 9.1 and 9.2.

2 Check that students are familiar with the language practised in the extra activities on pages 13 and 17.

3 Collect materials needed, for example old clothes, art materials, cardboard, sequins, an alarm clock, etc.

In class

Activity C: Costumes

The role of the costume people is to collect information and persuade other students to bring in their old clothes. They need to draw pictures of each character and (working with the whole class) decide what the characters will wear. Then, they should go around and see if anybody has anything suitable. For example, Hermia could be dressed in a long blue dress. It is likely that somebody in the class would have a long blue dress that they would be willing to bring in for the production. In any case, it is having a costume that is important, rather than the details. In addition, it is the process of designing the costumes that will enable people to practise their English. Finally, they should also be responsible for cutting out, decorating and fitting a donkey mask, as used in the play by Lysander.

Activity D: Props

* The first thing the props people should do is to read through the play carefully and compile a list of what props are needed. There are not all that many – a crown, some swords, an alarm clock, perhaps a magic wand for Puck.

* The props then need to be either found (around the school, at home, etc.) or made.

* The crowns can be easily made by drawing the shape on a flat piece of card, cutting them out, trimming them to the size of Theseus' and Oberon's heads and then decorating them with glitter, sequins, coloured pen, etc.

* Students can make the swords in a similar way. They should draw a sword on stiff card and then cut it out and cover it with silver foil. The handle of the sword will probably need to be reinforced with several layers of card (otherwise, during the sword fight between Lysander and Demetrius the swords tend to come apart).

Variation

An additional (optional) idea is to have somebody playing various extracts from popular songs at appropriate moments. For example, when Helena says *'But I love you, Demetrius'* in scene 2, a short clip of a well-known group singing a contemporary love song can be quite funny. It is a useful listening exercise for the people working on it, as they have to go through several contemporary songs to find just the right excerpt, record that clip onto a master-tape and then fit it in exactly with the correct moment of the play.

Topic area
theatre, stories, drama

Language focus
direct speech

Key vocabulary
duke, palace, sword, fairy,
mischief, cruel, execute,
chewing gum, sweetheart,
carrot, silly, dress rehearsal

Skills
speaking (See extra
activity page 17.)
writing

Level
intermediate or a mixed-
ability class

Time
each performance will
last about 25 minutes

Materials
as prepared in 9.3
video camera
art materials (for making
programme and poster)

9.4 The performance

Dress rehearsal

It is always a good idea to have one final dress rehearsal with all the props, costume and set. This is also the time that a member of the behind-the-scenes crew can video the play without getting in the way of the audience.

Making a programme

A programme can be made by students with smaller roles. This can list the performers and have a couple of appropriate drawings. In addition, students can write a short paragraph about the production and about William Shakespeare using the information in 9.1 or, alternatively, for more advanced groups, looking at the Shakespeare website at (http://www.stratford.co.uk/bard1.html). The programme can then be photocopied for handing out at the performance. Other students make posters to advertise the show (see below).

Who to invite

This depends very much on where you are. It is important to invite someone to see it, if only another class. On a short residential course, it is a good idea (if there is the space) to invite the whole school. In students' home countries, where students have classes on different nights, perhaps invite all the other people who are in the school on that night and advertise for others who might like to turn up.

Finally, don't forget to invite the parents; they always love the show, especially if the students make invitations the week before.

The performance

The performance is always a lot of fun. Try to get the students not to hurry through it because they are nervous. Behind-the-scenes people can hand out the props or stand at the door, handing out programmes and showing people to their seats. They can all watch when they are not performing.

A MIDSUMMER NIGHT'S DREAM

by William Shakespeare
adapted by Matt Wicks

CAST / CREW

NARRATOR /nərˈeɪtə/
(the narrator can also play any other part)
THESEUS /ˈθiːsiːəs/ (the king) *
HERMIA /ˈhɜːmiːə/ (Helena's sister)
LYSANDER /laɪˈsændə/
DEMETRIUS /dəˈmiːtriːəs/
HELENA /helˈeɪnə/ (Hermia's sister)
PUCK /pʌk/ (fairy)
OBERON /ˈəʊbərən/ (another king) *

PROPS   (1–3 people)
SET   (1–3 people)
COSTUME   (1–3 people)
SONGS   (1–4 people)
DIRECTOR   (1 person)

* Theseus and Oberon can be played by the same actor.
Note In a small class, the actors can do the behind-the-scenes jobs too.

NARRATOR: Welcome to our story, our little play. This is the tale of love, known as *A Midsummer Night's Dream*. Our story begins in the real world, in the Palace of _____ *1*. _____ *2* is King of our country, and everybody has forgotten how to speak _____*3*...

SCENE ONE
[Enter King THESEUS.]
THESEUS: Oh what a lovely day! I feel like going to _____ *4*.
[He sits on his throne. HERMIA, LYSANDER and DEMETRIUS enter.]
HERMIA/LYSANDER/DEMETRIUS: Good morning, Duke Theseus!
THESEUS: Good morning, my good and honest people. Hermia! You look so sad. What is the matter?
HERMIA: Oh wise and handsome Duke. This man, Demetrius, has agreed to marry me, because my father wants him to. But I am not interested. I am completely in love with this other man, Lysander. He is such a lovely man!
THESEUS: Hermia: you have to marry Demetrius.
HERMIA: Why should I?
THESEUS: Because your father wants you to! If you do not agree to marry Demetrius within two days, I will execute you.
DEMETRIUS: Please think about it, Hermia.
HERMIA: No.
DEMETRIUS: This is your fault!
LYSANDER: But I love her.
THESEUS: You have two days, no more! Come on, Demetrius.
[Exit THESEUS and DEMETRIUS.]
HERMIA: Oh, my only love, what shall we do now?

LYSANDER: I have a wonderful idea. I have an aunt who lives a long way away from here. She has a villa in the forests near _____ *5*. Let's run away together and stay with her. We can get married there and nobody will ever find us.

[Enter HELENA.]

HERMIA: Beautiful Helena, my dear sister. How are you?

HELENA: Oh, Hermia, I am so so sad. Demetrius loves you but I love Demetrius.

LYSANDER: This is very complicated.

HERMIA: I am always horrible to Demetrius.

HELENA: I know, but that only makes him love you more and more.

HERMIA: Don't worry. After tomorrow you will have no more problems. Lysander and I are going to run away to _____ *6* and leave this life behind.

[Exit LYSANDER and HERMIA.]

HELENA: At last! I have a plan to make Demetrius love me! I will tell him that his sweetheart is running away. He will understand that she does not love him, and he will love me. Me!

SCENE TWO

[The forest near _____*7*]

NARRATOR: Helena tells Demetrius all about Hermia, but Demetrius does not fall in love with her. He rushes off northwards following Lysander and Hermia to _____*8* ...

[DEMETRIUS enters, running. He stops and looks around him. A few seconds later, HELENA enters, also running.]

DEMETRIUS: I don't love you, so stop following me! I want to find Lysander and Hermia, so that I can kill Lysander with my sword! Go away!

HELENA: But I love you, Demetrius!

DEMETRIUS: Well, I think you are very ugly, and I don't love you at all.

[DEMETRIUS runs off.]

HELENA: I don't care. I'll follow you for ever.

[HELENA runs after him. After a few seconds, LYSANDER and HERMIA enter.]

HERMIA: Oh, Lysander, please stop. I am so tired.

LYSANDER: I know, my love. So am I. We have been walking for three days.

HERMIA: We're lost, aren't we?

LYSANDER: Well, yes. I can't actually remember where my aunt lives.

HERMIA: Can we rest?

LYSANDER: A very good idea.

HERMIA: You lie there and I'll lie here. I'll set the alarm clock for seven thirty.

LYSANDER: OK. Goodnight, Hermia. _____ *9*.

[They lie down apart and go to sleep.]

[PUCK enters, laughing madly.]

PUCK: Through the forest I have gone
But laughter, I found none.
Everyone seems sad today.
No-one even wants to play.
My name is Puck, I am a magic fairy with a hundred special powers, The thing that makes me very, very happy is to be very very naughty. There is a word in English: *mischief*. I am the king of mischief. At school, I steal other children's tests and put chewing gum on the teacher's chair. At home, I watch my mother making _____ *10* and then feed it to the cat. Watch carefully now, as I do some magic mischief on this sleeping man . . .
ABRACADABRA!

[PUCK waves his hands in the air above LYSANDER.]

Now, when he wakes up, he will fall in love with the first person he sees.

[PUCK laughs loudly and runs off.]

[LYSANDER and HERMIA turn over in their sleep. DEMETRIUS and HELENA enter, running.]

HELENA: Stay with me!

DEMETRIUS: Leave me alone.

HELENA: I cannot. My heart is yours.

DEMETRIUS: Oh no.

HELENA: Who is this? Lysander! He looks hurt, but I cannot see any wounds.

[LYSANDER wakes up. He stares at HELENA. DEMETRIUS runs off. HERMIA slowly begins to wake up.]

LYSANDER: Oh Helena ... you are so beautiful. I love you so much.

HELENA: Pardon?

LYSANDER: I love you with all my heart.

HELENA: Don't be stupid, Lysander. What about Hermia? I thought you loved her.

LYSANDER: No, Hermia is ugly and boring and she supports _____*11*. It is you I love.

HELENA: You are completely mad! Demetrius! Demetrius, my love, where are you?

[HELENA runs off after DEMETRIUS.]

LYSANDER: No, don't go. Wait for me!

[LYSANDER runs off after HELENA. HERMIA, now fully awake, is left all alone and very upset.]

HERMIA: Oh, Lysander … How could you be so horrible to me. Don't leave me all alone here with a broken heart …

SCENE THREE

[The forest near _____ *12*]

NARRATOR: The loving couples run about in the forest. They are always arguing, and they are always watched by the naughty Puck and his King, Oberon …

[Enter OBERON and PUCK.]

OBERON: I am Oberon, King of all the fairies.

PUCK: [bows] My lord.

OBERON: Why are you laughing, Puck?

PUCK: Oh, just some little games, my lord. I cast a spell upon a man, who lay upon the ground. His heart has fallen deeply now For the woman he first found.

OBERON: Puck … you are in big trouble.

PUCK: Er … does it help to say I'm sorry?

OBERON: You have got forty-eight hours to make everything good again, or I will execute you.

[OBERON exits.]

PUCK: Oh no. Oh no. Poor Puck. Poor Puck. Poor Puck!

[PUCK exits. After a few seconds, DEMETRIUS and HERMIA enter.]

DEMETRIUS: Hermia, I just don't understand why you are so angry with me.

HERMIA: Where is Lysander? Why did he behave so strangely? Have you killed him?

DEMETRIUS: If I had him here, I would kill him. But, I promise you, my sweetest rose, my most beautiful star, that I did not kill him.

HERMIA: Then tell me where he is!

DEMETRIUS: I do not know.

HERMIA: You are an evil monster and I think you are the worst man in the world. Never look at me again.

[HERMIA exits.]

DEMETRIUS: My heart is heavy. Oh, so so heavy. I was wrong about Hermia, she is not the beautiful goddess that I thought she was. I am so sad that I am going to lie down here and die.

[DEMETRIUS lies down. After 30 seconds, HELENA and LYSANDER enter.]

LYSANDER: Why don't you believe me when I say that I love you?

HELENA: Because you have always loved Hermia.

LYSANDER: Oh, her, Demetrius can have her. I want you.

HELENA: You are just joking with me: treating me badly!

[DEMETRIUS stands up.]

DEMETRIUS: Lysander! Leave Helena alone, she is a good woman, and you behave terribly to her.

LYSANDER: Don't worry, Demetrius, I love Helena now. You can marry Hermia.

DEMETRIUS: No, No. I loved Hermia. Past tense. Now, she has rejected me and been horrible and cruel. I understand that I should love Helena and give her all my heart.

LYSANDER: But Helena is mine!

HELENA: No, I'm not.

[HERMIA enters.]

HERMIA: Oh, Lysander!

LYSANDER: Oh no!

HERMIA: [Holds LYSANDER's arm] How could you be so cruel to me?

HELENA: To you? He is being cruel to me!

LYSANDER: Let go of me. I hate being held by you. I don't want to marry you any more. I want to marry beautiful Helena.

[LYSANDER takes HELENA's arm.]

HELENA: Let go of me!

DEMETRIUS: Let her go!

[DEMETRIUS draws his sword.]

HELENA/HERMIA: No!

[LYSANDER draws his sword.]

LYSANDER/DEMETRIUS: Die!

[LYSANDER and DEMETRIUS start to fight. Eventually they exit, fighting. HERMIA and HELENA follow.]

SCENE FOUR

NARRATOR: Our young heroes fight for hours and hours until they are exhausted. Though still very angry, they lie down and fall asleep …

[LYSANDER, DEMETRIUS and HERMIA enter and go to sleep. PUCK enters and looks at them.]

PUCK: At last, these four young sweethearts are fast asleep, hidden in the forest deep. Oberon will cut off my head if I cannot make them all happy once again. But – Poor Puck! – I cannot remember all the magic words.

[PUCK opens his magic book and looks at it.]

Aha! Perhaps this spell will work:

MERISTOPHASKY!

[He waves his hands over HERMIA and LYSANDER. LYSANDER wakes up and starts to groan as his head turns into a donkey's head.]

LYSANDER: Eeeeyore.

[HERMIA wakes up.]

PUCK: Oh no.

HERMIA: Oh! What a strange dream I had. I wonder where I am …

[She sees LYSANDER.]

But who is this?

LYSANDER: Eeeyore. Eeyore.

HERMIA: What a beautiful voice, and what a handsome man. I wonder what his name is.

LYSANDER: Eyore! Eeeeyore!

HERMIA: Oh, come here, beautiful man!

PUCK: Oh no! I have used the wrong spell. What have I done now?

HERMIA: You have such beautiful ears.

[PUCK looks through his spell book again.]

PUCK: Oh dear, perhaps this one will work …

ABRACADABRAZINHO!

[HERMIA holds her head as the spell begins to work. LYSANDER makes a loud noise and collapses, returning to human form. PUCK runs out. DEMETRIUS wakes up. HELENA comes in, having just woken up.]

HELENA: I had such an odd dream.

DEMETRIUS: Me too.

LYSANDER: And me, it was all about carrots … Hermia, can you ever forgive me for what I said about you?

DEMETRIUS: And Helena, can you love me, even now when I have been very, very silly?

HELENA/HERMIA: Of course I can.

[They all leave.]

NARRATOR: And they all lived happily ever after … except Puck, of course …

[Enter PUCK and OBERON.]

PUCK: Everything is good again, my lord.

OBERON: I can see a happy life for them all in _____*13* , with good jobs as English teachers.

PUCK: And me, what about my future?

OBERON: We will see, Puck, we will see.

PUCK: Oh dear.

[They exit.]

THE END

FOOTNOTES

1 Put the name of a famous castle or palace here.

2 Put the name of a famous king (or queen).

3 Put the name of the most commonly spoken language in your class.

4 Put the name of a very beautiful beach or beauty spot here.

5 Put a local town near a forest if possible.

6 See 5 above.

7 See 5 above.

8 See 5 above.

9 Replace with a translation of 'goodnight' in the most commonly spoken language of the class.

10 A traditional dish of the country you are in.

11 A football team popular with the class.

12 See 5 above.

13 Put the name of the town/city that the students are studying in.

10 Time capsule

LEVEL: Pre-intermediate +

USING THIS PROJECT: The Time capsule is designed to be done as a complete project and cannot easily be broken down into 'mini-projects'. Because of this, whilst it is possible to omit or add things, the overall sequence needs to be followed.

Since the aim of this project is for students to bury all their work, it is important that they keep a scrapbook of their efforts. Each student (or you) should photocopy what they have done each lesson and put it in their scrapbook, before burying the capsule. This not only acts as a record, it also gives them something to take away with them at the end of the project. 10.3 gives a list of the sort of activities you can use in order to fill the time capsule. These activities can by done in any order and many can be done simultaneously by different groups allowing students to move from one to another as they complete a task.

	10.1 Introduction	10.2 Decisions	10.3 Filling the capsule	10.4 Burial
SKILLS	• speaking	• speaking	• writing • reading • speaking	• speaking • writing
TIME	60 minutes	20–30 minutes	A: 45 minutes B: 30 minutes C: 30 minutes + 15 minutes in subsequent lessons D: 60 minutes E: 5 minutes per student F: 90 minutes	30 minutes
PREPARATION	• filling a box with things from the past	• photocopying	A–B: none C–D: photocopying E: get students to bring in pictures F: finding pictures • photocopying	• finding a suitable place to dig a hole
CLASS SIZE	3 plus	3 plus	2 plus	2 plus
PAGE NUMBER	118	119	121	127

Topic areas
history, people, countries

Language focus
modals of deduction
past tenses

Key vocabulary
time capsule, headlines, various as dictated by the contents of the box (diaries, recordings, etc.)

Skills
speaking

Level
pre-intermediate +

Time
60 minutes

Materials
large box
artefacts from the past

10.1 Introduction

Before class

1   Find a large box, preferably one that you can lock or seal in some way. This will be your time capsule. You will then fill it with various 'artefacts' from the past. These do not all need to be genuine historical items. Examples of things to include are: photos (of people and the area), old maps (from tourist offices or photocopied from history books), newspapers (real papers from 20 years ago – your local library will often have these – or more contemporary newspapers with the date cut off), letters (again, real or imaginary), recordings of music of the time that the capsule is supposed to have come from, recordings of people's voices (probably acted by other members of staff), diaries (copy out a couple of pages of a published diary such as Anne Frank's, for example), a list of predictions written (supposedly) years ago about what the author thought would have happened in the world by now. You could also include a few objects with no apparent use today (a box with a hole in it, for example, or a small piece of glass with a sign saying 'This way up' attached to it).

2   Once the box is reasonably full, seal it with a large sticker on the front saying DO NOT OPEN UNTIL . . . (today's date).

In class

1   Take the box into the class and tell students that this is a time capsule. It was buried 25 years ago and has just been dug up. They guess what is inside.

2   Make a list on the board of all their ideas.

3   Then open the box with the class and start to bring out the objects one by one. The students, in small groups, have to work out either what the object is, or what the story behind the photo / headline is.

   *   With the unusual objects the students in groups of three or four can touch them and guess their function (the box with a hole is a camera, the glass a child's microscope).
   *   With the photos, students in twos or threes deduce what is happening and who the people are.
   *   With newspaper headlines, students in larger groups (fives) make up a story which explains the headline (remembering that it took place 25 years ago).
   *   With recordings, students can try to imagine who this person was and what they were talking about.
   *   Diary entries can lead to interesting speculation – students can write what happened to the people after the extract that was in the box.
   *   With the predictions, students can say which ones have come true and which they think might yet come true.
   *   If you include pictures showing outdated fashions, you can then group the class (into fours) and give each one a picture. Ask them to produce a short description of the clothes they see. Collect the pictures, descriptions and any unused pictures and mix them up. Give each group another group's description and ask them to match it with the correct picture. Next, get them to check with the 'author group' if they were correct and, if not, to discover which bit of the description misled them.

4   Once the box is empty and the students have worked out what everything is, explain to them that this is what a time capsule is: a box which is buried and left for the future, as a record and a message.

5   Now tell the students that they are going to make a time capsule in the next lesson.

Topic areas
history, people

Language focus
making suggestions

Key vocabulary
time capsule, chart,
items which might go in
a time capsule (but see
10.1)

Skills
speaking (See page 17
for extra activity.)

Level
pre-intermediate +

Time
20–30 minutes

Materials
photocopy 1 x page
120 per student
photocopy and enlarge
1 extra copy of page
120

10.2 # Decisions

Before class

1 Photocopy page 120 for every student.

2 Photocopy and enlarge one more copy of page 120.

3 Complete 10.1.

In class

1 Make sure that students are familiar with the language connected with speaking activities (see page 17).

2 Having created an interest in time capsules with 10.1 Introduction, explain that the class is going to put together their own 'time capsule' to be opened in 2025 (or a date selected by the class). Tell them that it will be buried somewhere locally (or, if this is not possible that it will be locked away in a dark cupboard) until that date.

3 Put the class into small groups and get them to brainstorm ideas for things to put in the box. Examples of ideas that are often suggested include pictures of famous people, diaries, stories, recordings of songs / speaking, posters, drawings, examples of their work, clothing, photos of football programmes, etc. After about ten minutes, bring the groups together and get the students to report back on what they have thought of.

4 Write each new idea on the board as they come up.

5 The class then votes on which of these ideas they wish to do for their box. Each student then writes down the class choices on their 'CAPSULE PLAN' by filling in the blanks on photocopiable page 120. Put an enlarged version on the wall for everybody to see each time they enter the classroom.

6 Students must now volunteer for the parts of the project they wish to start on. Put the class into small groups or pairs.

7 Tell the pairs/groups that they should decide which section of the time capsule they would like to start work on and then negotiate with other groups until everybody reaches an agreement. Tell them that they will have the opportunity to do many different things during the course of the project so if they cannot do what they want straight away, they can do it later.

8 One student should be nominated as the person responsible for compiling a list of telephone numbers, names and/or addresses of the students for the box, so that when (if) it is dug up in 25 years they can be contacted. Younger students are very often taken with the idea that their own children might be able to come back and dig it up.

CAPSULE PLAN

From *Imaginative Projects* by Matt Wicks © Cambridge University Press 2000 **PHOTOCOPIABLE**

10.3 Filling the capsule

Topic area
A: geography
B: the future, jobs

Language focus
A: adjectives and spatial prepositions
B: the future

Key vocabulary
A: words to describe local area (e.g. *river, house, farm, field, hedge, lane, road, street, shops, light, bridge*, etc.)
B: names of jobs (e.g. *secretary, manager, bus driver, hairdresser, tourist guide*, etc.)

Skills
A and B: writing

Level
A and B: pre-intermediate

Time
A: 45 minutes
B: 30 minutes

In class

Activity A: Descriptions

1 Students write a short description of the area they live in. This should be quite detailed and geographical. Remind them that when the box is opened, the area will probably have changed quite a lot, so detail is very important. They can illustrate their descriptions as well, if they choose, with drawings, photographs and/or maps.

2 If two or more students live very close to one another (or if they are describing the school) one of them can write the basic text, and then the second can edit it, adding comments, e.g. *'Yes, I agree, it is very beautiful'*, or *'No, I think that this place is no good.' 'Don't forget the oak tree.'* etc.

3 Photocopy the descriptions for the students' scrapbooks and put the originals in the box.

Variation

For students studying in an English-speaking country, this can be done as an orienting activity on the first day so that students learn about their surroundings.

Activity B: Ambitions

1 Students work in small groups. Each student writes down on a piece of paper the sort of job that they imagine they will be doing in 2025, and also states why. If they say that they don't know, or have no idea, then tell them that they can invent something – perhaps they could be a film director, a film star, a model, etc.

2 The paper is then folded, named outside and handed to another group. The students in the other group write their predictions about what the authors will be doing in 2025, without looking at the first students' sentences.

3 The original students get their paper back and can see what predictions have been made. They write a sentence under the new predictions commenting on how they feel about them.
An example: The student's original sentence might have been *'I will be a famous actress because I like being in plays.'* One of her colleagues might have written *'I think Julianna will be a doctor because she is intelligent.'* Julianna would then write *'I disagree. I am not interested in being a doctor.'* If they agree, their sentence should be completed with an explanation, e.g. *'I agree. I like helping people.'*

4 Photocopy the predictions for the students' scrapbooks and put the originals in the box (with names clearly marked).

Topic areas
C: stories, feelings, holidays
D: people, jobs

Language focus
C: past simple / present perfect
D: question forms

Key vocabulary
C: *ski, crash, headache, poison, shy, date, to ask someone out*
D: none

Skills
C: writing, reading
C and D: speaking (See page 17.)

Level
C and D: pre-intermediate +

Time
C: *Lesson 1:* 30 minutes; 10–15 minutes each lesson after that
D: 60 minutes

Materials
C: 1 x pages 123 and 124 per pair
books to use as diaries
C and D: student scrapbooks
D (optional): tape recorder and microphone

10.3 Filling the capsule

Before class
(Activity C)
Photocopy one page 123 and one page 124 per pair.

In class

Activity C: Diaries

1 Make sure that all the students are familiar with the language connected with speaking activities (see page 17).

2 Put the students into pairs and give Student A a copy of Jake's Diary (page 123) and Student B a copy of Sally's Diary (page 124). Give them a few minutes to read the text.

3 Students then begin asking each other about the missing days (without letting their partner read their text). The questions can be as precise or vague as they like. (*'What did you do on Sunday?' 'Did you go to the cinema on Wednesday?' 'Who with?'*) Students may embellish, but cannot change the details in the text. They should be encouraged not just to read the text to their partner, but to paraphrase.

4 At the end of the exercise, the two students should both have completed diary entries for the week.

5 Now get the students to write their own entry for today. Encourage them to use the extracts as a model and warn them that their completed diaries will be placed in the time capsule.

6 Students write a regular diary for the length of the project. Every lesson each student has ten minutes to write about the events of the previous day. This can be used as a way of quietening a rowdy class. Alternatively, it can be done when students have finished one activity or have a short time to fill.

7 Correction should be given if students ask, but otherwise the integrity and privacy of the diary should be respected in order to make it as authentic as possible.

8 Put the diaries in the box (but let them photocopy the diaries so that they have a copy of their work).

Activity D: Interviews

1 Make sure that all the students are familiar with the language connected with speaking activities (see page 17).

2 Students choose who they are going to interview (the teacher, fellow students or someone else in school) and prepare some questions.

3 Check through the questions with the student(s). Ensure they keep the project aim in sight, and record life as accurately as possible. Encourage them to make the questions general (*'What do you think about the town that you live in?'*) rather than specific.

4 Send the students off to do the interviews. These can either be simple written questionnaires, or recorded conversations where enough tape recorders are available.

5 If the interview has been recorded, play it back to the students twice, first for pleasure, then to correct their pronunciation / grammar errors. If questionnaires were used, ask students to read them and correct orally.

6 Make copies of the tapes or questionnaires and add them to the box.

JAKE'S DIARY

Ask your partner questions to complete the blank dates.

Thursday 3rd January

I went to see Thomas today. Thomas is quite boring, but his sister is beautiful. In the afternoon, I went shopping with Sally, we bought some shoes and things, and then we went to the cinema to see the new James Bond film. Great film! (Sally hated it!)

Friday 4th January

....

....

Saturday 5th January

Sally is worse today. She says that it is the medicine I gave her yesterday.
Julia (Thomas' sister) asked me to go to the cinema with her tomorrow. It should be a good day!!

Sunday 6th January

....

....

Monday 7th January

Sally went to see Thomas today. I am still very angry! I spent all day packing my suitcase, because we are going to Switzerland tomorrow on a skiing holiday.

Tuesday 8th January

....

....

Wednesday 9th January

A terrible day! I broke my leg skiing down the mountain. I was trying to ski faster than Sally, but she stopped to get a coke. I couldn't stop and crashed. I was very embarrassed because Sally had to carry me back up the mountain. Now I have to spend three days in hospital.

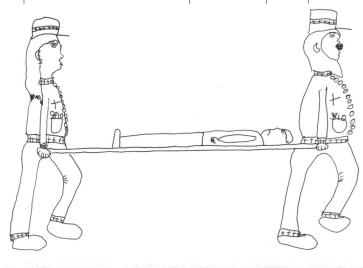

SALLY'S DIARY

Ask your partner questions to complete the blank dates.

Thursday 3rd January

....

....

Friday 4th January

I have been very ill today. I woke up with a terrible headache. (I think it was from the film!) I spent all day in bed, just reading about the holiday. I hope I get better before we go. Jake went out on his bike today and came back with some medicine for me. It is terrible. I think he has made a mistake and bought poison.

Saturday 5th January

....

....

Sunday 6th January

A wonderful day. I am so happy. Julia asked Jake to meet her in the cinema. When he got there she told him that she didn't really want to meet him. She was only there because Thomas (her brother) wanted to ask me out, but he is too shy. Jake came home (very angry) and told me about it. I phoned Thomas immediately. We are going on a date tomorrow!!!!

Monday 7th January

....

....

Tuesday 8th January

Today we travelled to Switzerland. I was very sad to say goodbye to Thomas (but it is only for one week!). We got to Zurich at 3pm and immediately took a bus up the mountain. Jake was sick on the aeroplane. When we arrived, he wanted to ski at night, but he cannot ski very well so we stopped him.

Wednesday 9th January

....

....

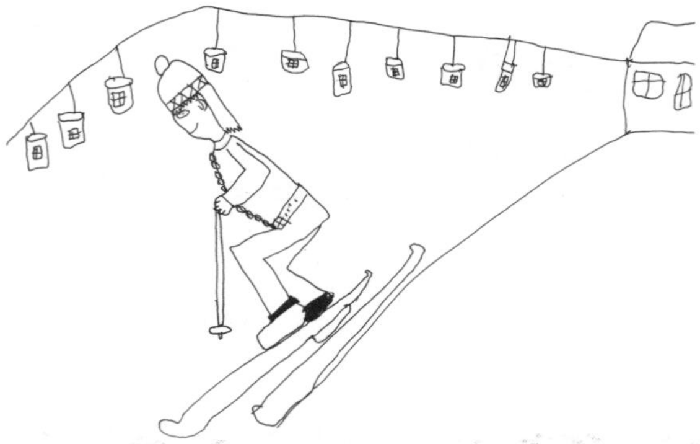

From *Imaginative Projects* by Matt Wicks © Cambridge University Press 2000 **PHOTOCOPIABLE**

Topic area
E: stories, families, people
F: famous people

Language focus
E: narrative tenses
adjectives
F: past simple
present perfect

Key vocabulary
E: *foreground, background,*
and as needed for photos
F: *chat show, scrapbook,*
idol, stepmother, to train

Skills
E: speaking (See page 17.)
F: reading, speaking

Level
E: pre-intermediate
F: pre-intermediate +

Time
E: 5 minutes per student
F: 90 minutes (variable
depending on level and
materials)

Materials
E: students' photos
optional: student
scrapbooks
F: magazines,
pictures of famous people,
glue, scissors,
photocopy 1 x page 126
per student
student scrapbooks
(See page 13.)

10.3 Filling the capsule

Before class

(Activities E and F)

1   Tell all the students to bring in a photograph of themselves or their families which they will put into the capsule.

2   Gather as many magazines as possible, with pictures of famous people. You will also need glue and scissors. Photocopy one page 126 for each student.

3   If you need to, don't forget to book time on the Internet for your class.

In class

Activity E: My life in pictures

1   Collect in all the photos and then hand them out again, making certain that nobody gets their own. They can write their names on the back of the photo in pencil to help you out here.)

2   Each student then has to look at the picture that they have been given and explain what is happening and what has just happened.

3   As the student is speaking, the picture should be passed around so that other students can join in the activity. A lot of the description will be guesswork, but often students can deduce quite a lot.

4   The student to whom the photo belongs then tells the true version of the story before adding it to the box. Students may want to photcopy their photos and stick them in their scrapbooks.

Variation

If students are on a residential course and far away from home, you can take pictures around the school of other students doing things and then use these for the activity.

Activity F: Hero scrapbook

1   Make sure that all the students are familiar with the language connected with creating things (see page 13).

2   Elicit from the students who Madonna (the pop star) is.

3   Give students a copy of page 126, and tell them that it is a scrapbook about Madonna. They look at it and see what sort of information it contains. What information did they already know? What is new? What would they include if they were making one?

4   Now tell them that they are going to make a scrapbook for the capsule about somebody who is popular: an actor, actress, singer or sporting personality. They can work in pairs or threes and should use old magazines, encyclopaedias, and the Internet if available, to research the person and acquire pictures.

5   Once they have sufficient information, they compile everything into a booklet or a poster and add a prediction at the bottom ... what do they think this person will be doing in 2025?

6   Copy your students' material and put it in the box.

MADONNA FACTFILE

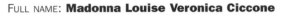

FULL NAME: **Madonna Louise Veronica Ciccone**

BORN: 16th August 1958, Michigan, USA

FAMILY: father, stepmother, 7 brothers and sisters.

MUSIC: Her first single was *Everybody.* Her first album was *MADONNA*; 2nd album: *Like a Virgin*; 3rd album *True Blue* (including *Papa don't preach*). She had to train her voice to be Eva Peron in *Evita.* Her most recent album is *Ray of Light.*

SOME FACTS AND FIGURES: She has recorded 12 albums, has had 29 Top Ten singles. Every album has sold over a million copies.

FILMS: *Desperately Seeking Susan, Dick Tracy, Truth or Dare, Evita, Shanghai Surprise*

'When I was very young
Nothing really mattered to me
But making myself happy.'

from: 'Nothing Really Matters' (*Ray of Light*)

PREDICTION:
In 2025, Madonna will not be making records any more. She will have a chat show in America.

10.4 # Burial

Topic area
history, ceremonies, geography

Language focus
prepositions of place

Key vocabulary
words to describe area where the box is to be buried
landmark, spade, dig, bury

Skills
speaking
writing

Level
pre-intermediate +

Time
30 minutes

Materials
paper for drawing and writing
a spade
student scrapbooks

Before class
Think about where you are going to bury the box and what sort of equipment you will need (usually just a spade).

In class

1 In order to complete the project, it would be nice to perform some sort of ceremony. This can simply be placing the items in the box, sealing and burying it. You could let the students bury the capsule, or invite a 'special guest'. They could prepare a short speech or a special sentence. In addition, perhaps they could plant a flower or shrub over the capsule.

2 Once the box has been buried, tell the students that they have to draw a detailed treasure map of the surrounding area, filling in landmarks and notes about, for example, what type of buildings there are, how far the hole is from the gate, etc.

3 This should form the final part of their scrapbook and the conclusion to the project.

Variation
* Students make a karaoke tape of their favourite songs.
* Students record a message to themselves in the future.
* Students write a secret in a sealed envelope which is then buried.
* Students make a plan of what they think their city will look like in 2025.
* Students alter photographs of themselves to show what they think they will look like in 2025.

Appendix 1: Using new technology

The Internet and computers are invaluable resources in project work, if they are used sensibly and not too often.

Generally, it is better to pre-select the sites that the students visit so as not to waste time.

Here are four suggested ways of integrating the Internet into project work:

*   Give students topics to research which are connected to the project. Make the topics quite specific (e.g., 'fashion in Brazil' rather than just 'fashion'). Start students at the Alta Vista website (http://www.altavista.com) because this accepts simple questions (e.g. 'Where can I find out about fashion in Brazil?').

*   Use the Internet as a bank of photographic resources. These can easily be printed out. For example, pictures of celebrity idols are needed in 6.1 or 10.3. Adverts can easily be found for 6.2 as well (Try http://www. (the name of the company).com or http://www.(the name of the company).co.uk)

*   E-mail can be used to communicate with ex-students and an E-mail exchange can be set up with schools in other countries.

*   With more experienced teachers and students, a quick and simple website on which students an display their work can be designed using Microsoft Front Pad (downloadable from http://www.microsoft.com).

Appendix 2: Using the community

The local community can offer two important things to classes engaged on project work: genuine interaction with native speakers, and a dimension of reality, which motivates students.

Here are four suggestions for taking the project out of the classroom:

*   Send students out to interview people. It can be a major part of the project or something extra. Almost all the projects have themes that people can be interviewed about e.g. their favourite film (project 2), places they like to travel to (3), their ideas on fashion (4), and so on.

*   Get students to find out about local amenities. In an English-speaking country, everything will, clearly, be in English. If not, the students translate this information into English for their presentations.

*   Try getting the local community into the school. Not only does this provide the school with publicity, it also motivates the students. It could be a showing of their film (2.4), their photo story (5.3), the whole exhibition (4), a performance of 'A Midsummer Night's Dream' (9). It doesn't matter who comes, parents, students from other classes, or others. You could also set up some kind of exchange with a local youth group.

*   [For students in English-speaking countries only]: Get students to go out and use what they have learnt. If they have studied travelling to Space City (3.3), get them to go to a travel agent, or to phone one up. For restaurants (project 7) get them to look at menus and compare prices.

Of course, all of these activities require good will and collaboration and so it is vital to warn people in advance. In addition, sending pairs into a shop is usually OK, but larger groups can cause problems.

Bearing these things in mind, though, the community is an excellent resource.